Stakeholder Theory
and Organizational Ethics

Robert Phillips

BERRETT-KOEHLER PUBLISHERS, INC.
San Francisco

Berrett-Koehler Publishers, Inc.
235 Montgomery Street, Suite 650
San Francisco, CA 94104-2916
Tel: (415) 288-0260 Fax: (415) 362-2512 www.bkconnection.com

ORDERING INFORMATION
Quantity sales. Special discounts are available on quantity purchases by corporations, associations, and others. For details, contact the "Special Sales Department" at the Berrett-Koehler address above.

Individual sales. Berrett-Koehler publications are available through most bookstores. They can also be ordered direct from Berrett-Koehler: Tel: (800) 929-2929; Fax: (802) 864-7626; www.bkconnection.com

Orders for college textbook/course adoption use. Please contact Berrett-Koehler: Tel: (800) 929-2929; Fax: (802) 864-7626.

Orders by U.S. trade bookstores and wholesalers. Please contact Publishers Group West, 1700 Fourth Street, Berkeley, CA 94710. Tel: (510) 528-1444; Fax (510) 528-3444.

Berrett-Koehler and the BK logo are registered trademarks of Berrett-Koehler Publishers, Inc.

Printed in the United States of America

Berrett-Koehler books are printed on long-lasting acid-free paper. When it is available, we choose paper that has been manufactured by environmentally responsible processes. These may include using trees grown in sustainable forests, incorporating recycled paper, minimizing chlorine in bleaching, or recycling the energy produced at the paper mill.

Library of Congress Cataloging-in-Publication Data
Phillips, Robert, 1968–
    Stakeholder theory and organizational ethics / Robert Phillips.
        p.   cm.
    Includes bibliographical references and index.
    ISBN 1-57675-268-2
    1. Corporate governance 2. Business ethics. I. Title.
    HD2741.P48 2003
    174'4—dc21   2003048112

Project Management: Shepherd Incorporated
Interior Design: Nancy Sabato

First Edition
08 07 06 05 04 03   10 9 8 7 6 5 4 3 2 1

CONTENTS

FOREWORD

Think about the recent headlines. Several who's who of American businesses have been dragged through scandal after scandal. Is there no ethics in business? Haven't business schools been teaching business ethics? Haven't the last 25 years of teaching and research in business ethics by philosophers and management thinkers made a difference? What's missing are a range of useful ideas and theories that managers can use to make better decisions. Robert Phillips has helped to remedy this situation with a very practical book.

He cuts through many vexing questions to propose a theory of organizational ethics that takes two important ideas seriously. The first is that organizations are dependent on their stakeholders for their successes and their failures. In fact he suggests that it makes little sense to talk about organizations in general and businesses in particular without paying careful attention to the essence of these stakeholder relationships. The second idea is the multifaceted theory of ethics from philosopher John Rawls and his followers. The heart of Rawls's view is his theory of justice articulated in the principle of equal liberty and the difference principle. The first admonishes us to take freedom seriously, a fact without which capitalism as we know it, is impossible. The second tells us that equality can't be left too far behind, a fact that we seem to have forgotten in recent times.

Phillips weaves a narrative of these two threads that tells an important story for business. Unlike the endless theorizing and counterexamples of philosophers, on the one hand, and unlike the mindless study of managerial opinion by "social scientists" on the other, Phillips suggests a point of view about business ethics that is at once normative and empirical. He grounds this point of view in the stakeholder literature and in Rawlsian ethics, and offers business ethicists a chance to escape their nineteenth-century intellectual prison fashioned by utilitarianism, Kant, and rights theory.

The heart of Phillips's argument is the notion that business needs to be based on an idea of fairness. Without fairness at the core, stakeholders will use the political process to hamstring economic activity—and rightly so in a just society. If executives come to base their decisions on Phillips's idea of fairness, or another well justified one, there can be little argument about justifying the regulation of economic activity.

Building new theory is sorely needed in this area, and theory of the pragmatic variety like this one, is on target. But, Phillips doesn't stop there. He shows how his ideas about fairness and stakeholders have practical consequences for the way that organizations treat certain stakeholder groups. According to Phillips, some are legitimate and others are merely instrumental (i.e., they can affect legitimate stakeholders, and so must be managed strategically). This question of legitimacy has many organizational implications for the identification and prioritization of key stakeholder groups.

Phillips joins a long line of distinguished management thinkers who have made "stakeholders" the centerpiece of their managerial mindset. He takes a well-deserved seat beside (1) the pioneers of the idea in its early days at the Stanford Research Institute (now SRI International), Igor Ansoff, Bob Stewart, Marion Doscher; (2) theorists such as Russell Ackoff, James Emshoff, Richard Mason, Ian Mitroff, Eric Rhenman, Fred Emery, and Eric Trist; and (3) contemporary thinkers such as Tom Donaldson, Lee Preston, Tom Dunfee, Jim Post, Tom Jones, Jeffrey Harrison, Donna Wood, Ron Mitchell, Brad Agle, Andrew Wicks, and others.

No theory is perfect, but as diverse people such as Immanuel Kant and Leonard Savage tell us, there is nothing so useful as a good theory. And, Phillips has produced a good one—both practical and well argued. One can't help but wonder whether we would have been treated to the current wave of scandals, as well as the hue and cry for more ethics in business, if Phillips's ideas were more widespread.

In short, read this book. Follow the argument. Think twice about what Phillips is saying to you and your organization. Figure out who are your legitimate stakeholders. Think about what it means to be fair to them, and for them to be fair to you. Engaging in this dialogue will make your business better. You will create more value and you'll do the right thing.

R. Edward Freeman
Charlottesville, Virginia
4 March 2003

PREFACE

Indeed, I must disclaim any originality for the views I put forward.

—John Rawls[1]

Though it is difficult to pin down with any precision the provenance of ideas, I believe I can trace the origins of this book to a late-fall day in 1994 under a tree on The Lawn at the University of Virginia—Mr. Jefferson's Academical Village. There are places in the world that simply feel like proper venues for scholarship; in the shadow of The Rotunda is such a place. There was a particular tree against which I would sit and read as I searched for a defensible moral foundation for stakeholder theory. I had come to Virginia's Darden School to study stakeholder theory and my interest in the work of John Rawls rendered it something of a foregone conclusion that the focus of my studies would involve the confluence of these two. In the fall of 1994, I was reading Donaldson and Dunfee's "integrative social contracts theory" articles and A. John Simmons's *Moral Principles and Political Obligations*. I took (still take) Donaldson and Dunfee's writings as exemplars for research in organizational ethics, but Simmons's critique of tacit consent and the social contract methodology is a powerful one—I was stuck. In another example of the great good fortune that has attended my studies, the Simmons book also contained an extended treatment of Rawls's principle of fair play. It was an epiphany. Here, under a tree on The Lawn I had found a locus for integrating those features that I believed necessary to a robust theory of organizational ethics. That day and the subsequent nine years have culminated in this book.

This book attempts to combine stakeholder theory and the moral and political theory of John Rawls into a single theory of organizational ethics. This task is both obvious and daunting for much the same reason: These theories can plausibly claim paradigmatic dominance in their respective fields. No approach to the examination of organizational ethics can claim a greater share of scholarly and popular attention than stakeholder theory over the past twenty years. No moral or political theory can claim greater twentieth-century influence than Rawls's *A Theory of Justice* and subsequent elaboration. I was stunned to hear Rawls's name uttered on television's *The West Wing* in February 2003. Think about the last time you heard the name of a contemporary political philosopher uttered on a top-ten network television program and you will have some idea of Rawls's influence.

A moment of reader guidance is perhaps called for here as the style of this book varies from chapter to chapter. The majority of the book can be understood by anyone familiar with the stakeholder concept while some of the material is quite dense and fairly technical. Understanding the technical and esoteric parts is not always necessary to understanding the remainder of the book, though leaps of faith may occasionally be required without such familiarity. The book is organized rather like a mountain—it is most accessible on the sides and is highest (in terms of the level of abstraction) in the middle. Chapters 1 and 2 should be palatable to academics and practitioners alike. An intuitive sense of the basic idea of a stakeholder and some of the attendant problems that can arise in the practice of stakeholder management are all that are required to appreciate these chapters. The same can be said of

Chapters 6 through 8. Chapters 6 and 7, about stakeholder legitimacy and the natural environment as a stakeholder, require slightly greater familiarity with the stakeholder debates, but are still well within the grasp of a reader who is not well versed in the academic literature. Chapters 3 through 5, on the need for an ethics of organizations, the main points of contention in the academic stakeholder literature, and the defense of the principle of stakeholder fairness, will be of most benefit to those already familiar with more academic treatments of business ethics and stakeholder theory—though Chapter 4 may also provide a good point of entry into the scholarly debates that currently swirl if one is interested in an overview of the state of the art in stakeholder theory. It is not necessary to climb to the summit of a mountain to appreciate it. One can see the entire mountain without going over the pinnacle and there is often practical value in doing so. But from my experience, there is also a certain satisfaction in attacking the summit. The perspective on the landscape below is far superior and the views from the base are given greater context and meaning.

For any project of such duration, one is bound to compile debts. Good fortune has brought me into contact with so much encouragement and assistance that my debts are still greater. Foremost among my academic debts are those I owe to Ed Freeman and Pat Werhane. Their contributions to my ideas on business, ethics, organizations, food, wine, leadership, writing, and myriad other subjects cannot be overstated. Whatever the merits of this book, they can claim the largest part of the credit. More than this, these two have provided a constant source of both personal and professional support. They are role models and friends.

I would also like to thank the many people who have seen fit to read and comment on earlier drafts of all or part of this work. In addition to providing a part of the original inspiration, A. John Simmons consented to participate on my dissertation committee and provided many useful comments on the ideas herein. Maureen Bezold, George Brenkert, Marty Calkins, the late Max Clarkson, Tom Donaldson, Tom Dunfee, Heather Elms, Paul Glezen, Douglas Hammer, Ed Hartman, Barry Johansen, Michael Johnson-Cramer, Tom Jones, Andrea Markowitz, Eric Orts, Lee Preston, Tara Radin, Joel Reichart, Richard Rorty, John Rowan, Tim Rowley, Gordon Sollars, Alan Strudler, Ann Svendsen, Harry Van Buren, Andy Wicks, and Don Yates have all commented on the ideas at least once and in most cases several times during the process. Joshua Margolis has been the most consistent source of criticism, stimulation, and encouragement on this book throughout the process—his efforts on behalf of the material contained here are unsurpassed and deserve special recognition. The book would doubtless be far better had I been able to address all of the concerns these insightful individuals suggested. Any remaining shortcomings in the book are despite rather than because of their input. This responsibility is my own.

There is no better place in the world to study organizational ethics than the University of Virginia, The Darden School, and the Olsson Center for Applied Ethics. I am grateful for their support. Similarly, I would like to thank the students, faculty, and administration of the University of San Diego for their support of the study and practice of ethics in all areas of life.

I would also like to thank the staff at Berrett-Koehler Publishers and especially Steve Piersanti and Jeevan Sivasubramaniam. The company is an exemplar of the stakeholder approach advocated herein. Working with them has improved both the form and the content of the book and I am proud of my association with them.

Finally and above all I want to thank my family. Hoyte Smith, Robert Pinkerton, and Eric Phillips have taught me in various ways the value of hard work, education, and intellectual achievement. Myrtle Smith, Una Mullis, and Amelia Phillips have reinforced these virtues with an infusion of complete and unconditional love. And before he was even a person, the idea of Smith Phillips provided motivation when nothing else could. This book is dedicated to him.

Robert Phillips
San Diego, California
8 March 2003

CHAPTER 1

Stakeholder Theory
and Organizational Dogma

B usiness organizations are among the most powerful social entities on earth. They are the grand social institutions of our time, perhaps the sole remaining effective social institutions, expected not only to fuel free-market economies, but also to carry burdens once thought the province of government and religion (e.g., health care, child care, protection of privacy, education). Business organizations control vast resources, cross national borders, and affect every human life. Their pervasive impact on human lives rivals that of history's most powerful czars, kings, and emperors.

Looking at the old cities of Europe gives one an idea of the movement of social power across time. The oldest of the large, elaborate buildings are religious in nature (e.g., churches and cathedrals). The second oldest of the large, elaborate buildings are governmental. The newest of the large, elaborate buildings are corporate headquarters and facilities.[a] To note this is to note the transfer of power through history. The church and its leaders were arguably the most powerful institution for thousands of

---

[a]This point was made by Roger W. Sant, CEO of AES Corporation, during a speech on the social responsibility of business.

years. Then, as the liberal notions of the Enlightenment began to replace church orthodoxy, government began to emerge as, again arguably, the most powerful institution on earth. Today, a case can be made that business firms are beginning to emerge as the most powerful institutions in the world.

Philosophy has generally kept pace with the historical transitions of power as described. Scholasticism preceded the giants of secular moral and political philosophy. Now, as power is transferred to business institutions and other private organizations, so must our theories recognize this transition in power and begin to look more closely, explicitly, and reflectively at the morality of economic interactions and the organizations where these transactions take place.

Business organizations are even taking on larger, more complicated roles in society. As they enter new arenas such as health care and education, where tough choices and trade-offs among multiple goods are commonplace, friction between economic objectives and other worthy aims is likely to increase. Elements of business and organizational ethics are interwoven within bioethics—the latter perhaps also a contender for the title of most important area of applied ethics.

If ethics is to become an integral part of business conduct, it must be knit into organizational life. Our theories must thus begin with a consideration of organizations. Just as scholars have previously attempted to philosophically analyze (and justify) the power wielded by the state and its agents, it is essential that at least a portion of our attention be turned to a philosophical analysis of the power wielded by managers in organizations.

Political and moral theory seeks a comprehensive explanation of ethical duties between moral agents. This level of abstraction is typically comprehensive and universal; that is, the classics of moral and political philosophy generally refer to all persons in all times and places. This book attempts to provide a general explanation of the creation and existence of moral obligations within organizations and among stakehold-ers.[b] As such, it is but one brick (although an important one) in the emerging edifice of stakeholder theory.

Stakeholder Theory

Organizations have constituencies. Furthermore, organizations are dependent upon these constituency groups for their suc-cess. This much is uncontroversial. Refer to these constituencies as stakeholders, however, and the disagreements appear cease-less. Who are these stakeholders? How should they be man-aged? Is there a legal duty to attend to stakeholders or is such a duty instead legally prohibited due to the shareholder wealth maximization imperative? Should the law require stakeholders on boards of directors? For whose benefit ought the organiza-tion be managed? Should stakeholder principles be extended to the entire world in pursuit of a stakeholder society?

The debate only becomes more intense when the ques-tions are couched in moral terms. What does the organization owe its stakeholders? Is there a moral obligation between the organization and its stakeholders? What is the source and jus-tification of this obligation? If the organization in question is a business organization, are there moral duties of any sort or is business either immoral or amoral in nature? The generally beneficial fact that everyone is an ethicist of a sort—having opinions and considered judgments about moral topics—only fuels the considerable fire when stakeholder theory is dis-cussed as a theory of organizational ethics. This book is an attempt to add some light to this heat.

Just as everyone is a sort of ethicist, so too is all activity in organizations, particularly business firms, shot through with

[b]This moral foundation would be analogous to the foundation provided by property rights in the neo-classical economics explanation of business. I will not, however, undertake to contrast the two concepts here except to say that the two are not mutually exclusive of one another. One may affirm property rights (although not to the degree of the neo-classical economist) and still affirm fairness-based obligations.

fodder for moral reasoning (more on this metaphor momentarily). R. Edward Freeman (1994) has identified and described a "separation thesis" at work in discussions of business. Academics and practitioners alike seem to operate with an underlying assumption that business is business and ethics is ethics, but the two have little if anything to do with one another. Professor Freeman argues that this is the greatest obstacle to moral decision making in organizations today.

It would have been easier five years ago to argue that accounting and finance are amoral. That is, they are neither moral nor immoral, but are instead not the sort of concepts to which application of moral ideas is appropriate. These fields of study and practice are merely tools for making decisions and are no more moral or immoral than a pen. Recent events have proven, however, clearly moral connotations to the use of these tools, just as with the use of pens. Anyone making the argument that the use of the tools of accounting and finance are amoral today would likely meet with stunned incredulity in light of recent events.

A still deeper variation of this argument, however, is even more dangerous. The assertion that the purpose of business activity is to maximize the wealth of the business's owners—shareholders in the case of corporations—has near religious status. It is the dogma of business and is taken for granted like the air we breathe. I examine this claim at some length in later chapters. For now, it is sufficient to point out that the prescription to maximize shareholder wealth is itself a moral claim rendered using the language of moral reasoning. The utilitarian variation says that individuals working toward their own self-interest will actually benefit society as a whole. Even when extended from individuals to organizations, the rationale for maximizing owner wealth lies in the benefits that accrue to society: "A rising tide lifts all boats" is a moral argument.

In addition to the utilitarian argument is the property rights argument, which says that because the shareholders own the firm, managers bear an obligation to act consistently with shareholders' wishes, assumed to be wealth maximization. Again, talk of property *rights* is moral reasoning. So, when Professor John Dienhart is asked how long ethics has been a topic of study in schools of business, his stock response is, "As long as there have been schools of business."[c] Merely assuming a moral stance without reflection does not make it any less a moral argument. One issue that arises from the uncritical acceptance of the shareholder wealth maximization model as the moral foundation of business activity is that responses to immoral behavior in such contexts also take this foundation for granted. Few of the fixes that have been suggested to avoid the problems that have recently plagued U.S. firms have directly addressed the shortcomings of this model.

An analogy to an idea in a Darwin Awards message is perhaps apt. A man is out hunting and upon trying to start his old truck to leave he realizes that he has blown a fuse. His idea for a replacement is a .22 caliber shell that is near to hand. The shell promptly fires off, wounding the man as he sits in the driver's seat. I rather doubt the truth of the story, but it strikes me that many of the solutions proposed to repair organizational ethics are akin to trying a different size shell. The problem is more fundamental than whether the shell is a .22 or a .25. We should not be surprised that, until this more fundamental problem is addressed, firms will continue shooting themselves in the foot, or worse.[d]

This book suggests that organizations in the early twenty-first century are confronted with a unique set of moral issues requiring moral theory explicitly tailored to this set of issues and that stakeholder theory is a strong candidate of such a theory of organizational ethics. This book will argue that an amended principle

---

[c]Personal correspondence, February 2003.

[d]To qualify as a Darwin Award winner, our protagonist necessarily had to have shot himself is an area rather more sensitive than the foot.

of fair play—the principle of stakeholder fairness—provides a defensible source of moral obligations among stakeholders that has been heretofore missing in the literature on stakeholder theory. The remainder of this chapter will be devoted to a broad summary description of what is to follow.

Chapter 2: The Limits of Stakeholder Theory

Much of the power of stakeholder theory may be attributed to its conceptual breadth. The term carries myriad connotations and thereby evokes praise or scorn from scholars and practitioners of multiple academic disciplines and backgrounds. Such breadth of interpretation, though one of stakeholder theory's greatest strengths, is also one of its most prominent theoretical liabilities. Much of the power of stakeholder theory is a direct result of the fact that, when used unreflectively, its managerial prescriptions and implications are nearly limitless. In the hands of advocates and critics alike, stakeholder theory can be used as a basis for nearly any position that one wishes to defend or attack. Wide conceptual breadth allows critics to dress up the theory as they will in the process of attempting to lay it low. In some cases, overzealous advocates may tend to make the critic's job easier as well. Chapter 2 elaborates a number of interpretations, critical and friendly, of stakeholder theory that do not represent the theory described in the current project. After a brief discussion of the nature of stakeholder criticism, I will argue for what stakeholder theory is NOT. With this brief summary as our roadmap, we may now proceed to describe and defend the concepts of organizational ethics in general and stakeholder theory in particular.

Chapter 3: Why *Organizational* Ethics?

Organizational ethics scholarship has historically consisted of attempts to directly translate the classics of moral and political theory into the context of the organization. Hence, the gamut includes utilitarian business ethics, Kantian business ethics, Aristotelian business ethics, and social contractarian business ethics. Many of these translations have been provocative, interesting, coherent, and insightful; however, many of the distinct qualities of organizations and the nuances of the moral problems that arise in organizational contexts are inadequately appreciated. Both moral and political philosophy are too broad and general to account for the obligations that arise in the myriad organizations (business and otherwise) of less than nation-state size and power. This being the case, the need arises for a normative account of organizational morality that, while grounded in the moral and political theories of the past, is tailored specifically for the organizational level of abstraction. Chapter 3 attempts to point out problems that may arise with the more or less direct translation of moral and political philosophical concepts and methodologies.

Having suggested reasons why moral and political philosophy may be inadequate in organizational contexts, Chapter 3 goes on to suggest features that would characterize an ethics of organizations including substantive aims and conceptual independence. With the need for specific theory at the organizational level established, I argue that stakeholder theory is a good candidate. To prepare the foundation for a defense of stakeholder theory, Chapter 4 is an extended discussion of the current status of stakeholder theory as a scholarly topic.

Chapter 4: Stakeholder Theory and Its Critics

Prior to any attempt to elaborate a new stakeholder theory, it is important to have a thorough understanding of past and current thinking about the concept. Chapter 4 attempts to survey the recent work in the field relevant to the topic at hand. Among the most important and widely cited papers in the area are those that suggest a variety of distinctions and taxonomies

among stakeholders and stakeholder research (e.g., Donaldson & Preston; Mitchell, Agle, & Wood; and Jones & Wicks).
These taxonomies and their role in the development of stakeholder theory are briefly analyzed.

From here the discussion moves to the topic of fiduciary
duties and agency relationships. Critics charge that stakeholder theory, particularly the prescription that managers
do otherwise than maximize shareholder wealth, violates
legal and moral duties. Far from being morally superior to
the status quo, critics charge that stakeholder theory advocates the violation of strong moral duties. Goodpaster's
(1991) explication of the "stakeholder paradox" exemplifies
this critique. He argues:

> It seems essential, yet in some ways illegitimate, to orient corpo-
> rate decisions by ethical values that go beyond strategic stake-
> holder considerations to multi-fiduciary ones.[2]

Such arguments rely heavily on the notions of the agency and
fiduciary duties of managers to share owners. Based on agency
considerations, the relationships between managers and shareholders are held to be "special" and ethically different from
other stakeholder relationships. The extent to which these
relationships are, in fact, "special" is examined.

Chapter 4 ends with a summation of the problems with
extant stakeholder research to be addressed in the remainder
of the book. Among these problems are the lack of a normative
justificatory framework and uncertainty regarding stakeholder
identity and legitimacy. That is, much of the current thinking
on stakeholder theory omits discussion of the normative,
moral justification for obligations to stakeholders. In addition
to the reasons provided above regarding business dogma, failure to address the normative foundation creates the problem
of stakeholder identity. Though some have addressed this
issue, it remains problematic that much of the extant thinking
on stakeholder theory is unable to distinguish those who are

from those who are not legitimate stakeholders: If everyone is a stakeholder, then the term is empty and adds no value.

The absence of a normative framework and the problem of stakeholder identity are among the theoretical shortcomings addressed by the principle of stakeholder fairness. The principle of stakeholder fairness—and its predecessor, the principle of fair play—are examined and explicated in Chapter 5.

Chapter 5: A Principle of Stakeholder Fairness

Chapter 5 provides an answer to, why managers should care about stakeholders. Beyond the financial reasons (and the moral rationale that underlies profitability) are other moral obligations that arise in organizational contexts. This chapter defends the principle of stakeholder fairness, which states that when people are engaged in a cooperative effort and the benefits of this cooperative scheme are accepted, obligations are created on the part of the group accepting the benefit. These obligations are elaborated, defended, and compared with other forms of obligation generation such as actual and implied consent.

The principle of stakeholder fairness only provides for the existence of obligations among stakeholders; the content of the obligations must be filled out within the particular contexts of organizational interaction. In other words, that there are obligations and who the parties to these obligations are is determined using the principle of stakeholder fairness. The content of these obligations (i.e., what the parties are obligated to do or refrain from doing) is established by the norms of the particular organization and its stakeholders. The proper test of the legitimacy of such norms is in the discussion of them among all of the parties to the norm. This discourse test for establishing the content of obligations of fairness is elaborated and examined. Chapter 5 concludes with a discussion of a decision made by Cadbury's as an example of communicative stakeholder management.

Chapter 6: Stakeholder Legitimacy

Among the problems with much of the stakeholder literature to date is the inability of previous theories to delimit those groups that are and those groups that are not legitimate stakeholders. It is argued that this is due to an insufficient understanding of the notion of legitimacy in stakeholder theory. Chapter 6 begins, therefore, by defending a multifaceted conception of legitimacy. It is argued that legitimacy in stakeholder theory can be separated into normative and derivative varieties. Normative legitimacy is created by the principle of stakeholder fairness and the obligations that arise there from. Derivative legitimacy is derived from these prior moral obligations and gets its force from the ability of certain groups to affect the well-being of the organization and its normative stakeholders. The vital category of non-stakeholder is also preserved. This distinction creates a conception of stakeholder legitimacy that is more consistent (both within the domain of stakeholder research and with stakeholder theory's disciplines of origin), is able to broadly suggest a moral and logical hierarchy for stakeholder groups, and keeps the moral aspects of the theory in view for decision makers.

Chapter 7: Stakeholder Identity

Facilitated by this new understanding of legitimacy in stakeholder theory, itself grounded in the principle of stakeholder fairness, we are now able to address the problem of stakeholder identity. That is, which constituency groups are normative, derivative, and non-stakeholders and why? By way of example, this new conception of legitimacy is applied to the media and competitors. It is then argued at greater length that neither the natural environment nor social activists are normatively legitimate stakeholders on a fairness-based account. The primary reason for this is the organization has accepted no benefits from these entities nor have these entities voluntarily contributed to the organizational cooperative scheme. The stuff of reciprocity is absent.

It is also argued, however, that these entities may be accounted for, both from within and external to the fairness-based stakeholder theory presented here. It is argued that stakeholder theory may account for these entities in at least two ways. If the activists are able to significantly affect the well-being of the organization and its normative stakeholders in either a positive or negative manner, then they may be considered derivative stakeholders meriting managerial attention. Also, if there is an interest in the activists' causes (or a vital interest in the natural environment even absent any activist representation) among legitimate stakeholders (e.g., the local community), then these groups may be considered as stakeholder proxies and achieve similar derivative status. In the case of social activists, similarities exist between this instrumental approach and the moral theory of civil disobedience. This relation between "stakeholder proxies" and civil disobedience is explored.

Finally, it is important in this context to recall that stakeholder theory is far from exhaustive of moral theory. A vast array of moral duties, rights, responsibilities, and obligations exist apart from stakeholder obligations. Therefore, an organization is precluded from taking actions vis-à-vis the natural environment or social activists apart from the stakeholder status of these entities. For example, the organization may have a duty to not unnecessarily harm the environment based on the moral considerability due non-human entities.

Chapter 8: Stakeholder Theory in Practice

Having completed the defense of stakeholder theory, the final chapter looks more explicitly at the implications of the theory for the practice of administration in organizations. How can this new version of stakeholder theory help address the most common challenges leveled against it from a practical perspective? How does it help manage for stakeholders? Chapter 8 will take the form of answering a series of interrelated questions that would naturally arise for a manager wishing to employ the theory.

1. In light of business dogma, why should I manage for stakeholders?
2. Knowing why I should manage for stakeholders, how do I know who the stakeholders are?
3. Knowing who the stakeholders are, how should I go about determining what they want?
4. Knowing what my stakeholders want but being limited in resources, how do I prioritize among all of these groups?
5. Are the rules of business truly different from other endeavors? If so, how?

Chapter 8 also suggests other resources for the reader in search of further practical advice as well as a number of challenges and questions to the theory that remain unanswered.

CHAPTER 2

The Limits of Stakeholder Theory

The term *stakeholder* is a powerful one due, to a significant degree, to its conceptual breadth. Because the term means many different things to many different people, it evokes praise or scorn from scholars and practitioners of myriad academic disciplines and backgrounds. Such breadth of interpretation, though one of stakeholder theory's greatest strengths, is also one of its most prominent theoretical liabilities as a topic of reasoned discourse. Much of the power of stakeholder theory is a direct result of the fact that, when used unreflectively, its managerial prescriptions and implications are nearly limitless. When discussed in its "instrumental" variation (i.e., that managers should attend to stakeholders as a means to achieving other organizational goals such as profit or shareholder wealth maximization), stakeholder theory stands virtually unopposed.[3]

This interpretive breadth has also provided a rich source of fodder for those critics of the theory who remain. The same wide-pattern sieve that has allowed business ethicists and social issues in management scholars to find whatever they were originally seeking from the theory has also admitted of criticisms that either do not or need not apply to stakeholder theory. This has created a situation in which it has been occasionally difficult to figure out who among those writing about the stakeholders are critics and who are advocates. Prominent theorists have criticized stakeholder theory only to later—in the same work—return to advocate some instrumental version of it.[4]

This chapter is the result of several sources of inspiration. The most obvious is the frequent recurrence of similar distortions within the critical literature and less formal discussions of stakeholder theory. The notion of strict stakeholder equality; application of the theory either to the entire economy or exclusively to large, publicly held corporations; and concerns with changes in the law and corporate governance are common in the literature among stakeholder theory apologists and critics alike. The other idea motivating this chapter comes from Donaldson and Preston's (1995) widely cited article. They argue that stakeholder research is "managerial," which, at first blush is a rather straightforward proposition, until one tries to unpack this notion. If the stakeholder theory is managerial, what does this imply that it is NOT?[a]

In many ways, defending stakeholder theory is a bit like shadow boxing. Owing in part to the ambiguity and breadth of stakeholder theory itself, critiques are often implicit. Many of the most common, and potentially damaging, criticisms of stakeholder theory have not, to my knowledge, been formally elaborated in the management literature. This chapter attempts, in addition to responding to some explicit critiques, to expose and address some of these implicit criticisms. Therefore, at a few points in the article, the reader might expect to see a citation indicating who has leveled the critique in question. The criticism in these cases represents an amalgam of fre-

---

[a]This is not to say that those pursuing stakeholder research in non-managerial areas (e.g., law and regulation or political economy) are doing so illicitly. I am merely proposing a set of limitations make the theory better able to answer one set of common critiques. Persons pursuing research in other areas will provide additional responses to these criticisms or fall victim to them.

quent and persistent critiques of stakeholder theory from my experience discussing stakeholder theory with scholars, students, and executives. Finally, some of the criticisms are my own as I myself am (perpetually) dissatisfied with the current state of the theory.

The goal of the current chapter is like that of a controlled burn that clears away some of the underbrush of misinterpretation in the hope of denying easy fuel to the academic arsonists and the critical conflagration that would raze the theory. The aim is to narrow the technical meaning of *stakeholder*[b] for greater facility of use in management and organizational studies. By elaborating a number of common misinterpretations of the theory, I hope to render a stronger and more convincing stakeholder theory as a starting place for future research.

What Stakeholder Theory Is

Before discussing what stakeholder theory is not, an outline of what stakeholder theory is would be helpful. Stakeholder theory is a theory of organizational management and ethics. Indeed all theories of strategic management have some moral content, though it is often implicit. This is not to say that all such theories are moral, as opposed to immoral. Moral content in this case means that the subject matter of the theories involves inherently moral topics (i.e., they are not amoral). For example, in arguing that current organizational arrangements and processes should be ignored as organizations are "reengineered," managers are asked to ignore existing relationships and obligations among organizational actors.[5] These obligations may be overcome by other stronger obligations, but that is a subject of moral discourse and if implied, should be exposed and examined. Moral content is frequently taken for granted, implied, or ignored in this manner in management scholarship.

---

[b]It is unrealistic to attempt to change or limit the use of *stakeholder* in the common parlance.

Stakeholder theory is distinct because it addresses morals and values explicitly as a central feature of managing organizations.[c] The ends of cooperative activity and the means of achieving these ends are critically examined in stakeholder theory in a way that they are not in many theories of strategic management. Stakeholder theory is conceived in terms that are "explicitly and unabashedly moral."[6] This is evidenced in the branch of stakeholder theory literature examining the moral foundations of the theory (see Table 1).

Managing for stakeholders involves attention to more than simply maximizing shareholder wealth. Attention to the interests and well-being of those who can assist or hinder the achievement of the organization's objectives is the central admonition of the theory. In this way, stakeholder theory is similar in large degree with alternative models of strategic management such as resource dependence theory.[7] However, for stakeholder theory, attention to the interests and well-being of some non-shareholders is obligatory for more than the prudential and instrumental purposes of wealth maximization of equity shareholders. While there are still some stakeholder groups whose relationship with the organization remains instrumental and derivative (due largely to the power they wield) there are other normatively legitimate stakeholders besides equity shareholders.

At its current stage of theoretical development, stakeholder theory may be undermined from at least two directions: critical distortions and friendly misinterpretations.[8] Some have sought to critique the theory based on their own stylized conception of the theory and its implications. Though not always without some textual evidence for such characterizations, I argue that many of these distortions represent straw-

[c]Certain studies done under the rubric of stakeholder theory are more descriptive or instrumental and rely on ends and values that are implicit or assumed. I argue that, although many such studies are quite useful, it is the explicit reference to moral language and acknowledgment of a moral foundation that make stakeholder theory distinct. Thanks to Thomas Jones for this point.

TABLE 1   Normative Justifications for Stakeholder Theory

Author	Normative Core
Argandoña (1998)	Common Good
Burton & Dunn (1996) Wicks, Gilbert, & Freeman (1994)	Feminist Ethics
Clarkson (1994)	Risk
Donaldson & Dunfee (1999)	Integrative Social Contracts Theory
Donaldson & Preston (1995)	Property Rights
Evan & Freeman (1993)	Kantianism
Freeman (1994)	Doctrine of Fair Contracts

person versions of the theory. At the least, the critical [mis]interpretations do not represent the strongest, most defensible variation of stakeholder theory. I will begin by discussing interpretations that have provided fodder for critics as well as alternative interpretations that make stakeholder theory more resilient to such attacks (see Table 2).

As mentioned, these distortions are not without some textual basis in the literature. However, stakeholder theory has also suffered at the hands of well-meaning, but perhaps overzealous, advocates. The wide-ranging intuitive appeal of stakeholder theory has led a number of scholars and commentators to stretch the theory beyond its proper scope, rendering it more susceptible to criticism and distortion. In the second part of the chapter I will address friendly misinterpretations that tend to weaken stakeholder theory.

Critical Distortions: Straw-Persons and Evil Genies

Finding fault with an existing theory or model is easier than creating and defending an alternative. The former activity is easier still, under two time-honored and widely used

TABLE 2   What Stakeholder Theory Is Not

Critical Distortions	Friendly Misinterpretations
Stakeholder theory is an excuse for managerial opportunism (Jensen, 2000; Marcoux, 2000; Sternberg, 2000).	Stakeholder theory requires changes to current law (Hendry, 2001a, 2001b; Van Buren, 2001).
Stakeholder theory cannot provide a sufficiently specific objective function for the corporation (Jensen, 2000).	Stakeholder theory is socialism and refers to the entire economy (Barnett, 1997; Hutton, 1995; Rustin, 1997).
Stakeholder theory is primarily concerned with distribution of financial outputs (Marcoux, 2000).	Stakeholder theory is a comprehensive moral doctrine (Orts & Strudler, 2002).
All stakeholders must be treated equally (Gioia, 1999; Marcoux, 2000; Sternberg, 2000).	Stakeholder theory applies only to corporations (Donaldson & Preston, 1995).

approaches to criticism. The first is the use of so-called straw-persons. A critic sets up the object of her criticism in such a way that it is easily felled by whatever rhetorical axe the critic happens to be wielding.

The other well-worn implement of criticism is that of holding the objectionable theory to a higher standard than that to which the proposed alternative is subjected. Sometimes this takes the form of what some call the evil genie (or evil genius, evil demon, or consistent deceiver) argument. An evil genie argument is one that is no more (or less) problematic for any one theory or idea than the extant alternatives. In the course of casting all knowledge into radical doubt, Descartes suggested that even ideas that appear true beyond doubt (e.g., $2 + 2 = 4$) may be mistaken. There may be an omnipotent deceiver (Malin Genie) that consistently leads one to believe that $2 + 2 = 4$ when in fact $2 + 2 =$ banjo. While an evil genie may exist, the existence of such a being is a problem for all theories and arguments equally. Critics of stakeholder theory use both tools rather liberally. Following are brief criticisms based on versions of the theory that are either outdated, distorted, or both, and alternative interpretations that should help overcome the objections.

Stakeholder theory is an excuse for managerial opportunism.

The shareholder wealth maximization imperative is frequently motivated by so-called agency problems: hazards arising from the separation of risk bearing and decision making (also known as ownership and control, respectively). The concern is that without this moral imperative, managers would enrich themselves at the expense of the organization and the recipients of its residual cash flows, the shareholders.

In the hope of mitigating such opportunism, a moral (and legal) argument is proffered regarding the obligations between shareholders and the board of directors. The separation of risk bearing and decision making is the problem; a moral and legal obligation on the part of the agent to act solely in the interest of the principal is the solution. Significantly, the interest of the principal is *assumed* to be exclusively wealth maximizing.

Rather than morally superior, therefore, stakeholder theory is actually immoral inasmuch as it ignores this agency relationship—or so goes the argument. This criticism is, however, the result of the overextended metaphor of agency theory in economics. If managers are agents or fiduciaries at all, it is to the *organization* and not to the shareowners (see Chapter 4). The corporation is not coextensive with the shareholders. It is an entity unto itself. It may enter into contracts and own property (including its own stock[d] or that of other

---

[d]We might test the proposition that shareholders own the corporation through a thought experiment: Who would own the corporation if it bought back all of its own stock?

corporations). It has standing in a court of law. Limited liability ensures that shareowners are not, in general, personally liable for the debts of the organization.[9] Top managers are agents for the corporation, which is not merely a shorthand way of saying that they are agents for the shareholders. The corporation is meaningfully distinct.[10] The same goes for other limited liability entities such as limited liability partnerships to the extent that it is the partnership that has legal standing separate from that of the partners themselves, and the partners enjoy immunity from personal responsibility for the actions and debts of the organization.

Some have suggested that stakeholder theory provides unscrupulous managers with a ready excuse to act in their own self-interest, thus resurrecting the agency problem that the shareholder wealth maximization imperative was designed to overcome. Opportunistic managers can more easily act in their own self-interest, by claiming that the action actually benefits some stakeholder group or other. "All but the most egregious self-serving managerial behavior will doubtless serve the interests of *some* stakeholder constituencies and work against the interests of others"[11] and by appealing to the interests of those who benefit, the manager is able to justify the self-serving behavior. Hence, stakeholder theory "effectively destroys business accountability . . . because a business that is accountable to all, is actually accountable to none."[12]

The first response to this criticism is to point out that no small measure of managerial opportunism has occurred in the name of shareholder wealth maximization. In addition to the debacles at Enron and WorldCom, one need only consider the now dethroned king of shareholder wealth, Al Dunlap, for an illustration.[13] Dunlap grossly mismanaged at least two companies to his own significant, if temporary, financial gain; and every move he made was in the name of shareholder wealth. Dunlap agreed to pay $15 million to settle a lawsuit brought by the shareholders of Sunbeam Corporation.[14] There is little reason to believe that stakeholder theory will provide any more or less justification for the opportunistic manager.

This criticism of stakeholder theory is a version of the evil genie argument. Managerial opportunism is a problem, but it is no more a problem for stakeholder theory than the alternatives. In their discussion of "stakeholder-agency" theory, Hill and Jones[15] argue that managers' interest in organizational growth (citing remuneration, power, job security, and status as motivating this interest) runs contrary not only to the interests of stockholders but also to the interests of other stakeholders. They write, "[o]bviously, the claims of different groups may conflict. . . . However, on a more general level, each group can be seen as having a stake in the continued existence of the firm."[16] Stakeholder theory, therefore, does not advocate the service of two masters. Rather, managers serve the interest of one master: the organization.

One could make a case that having to answer to multiple constituencies will increase accountability rather than mitigate it. That a manager can *attempt* to justify self-serving behavior by reference to some stakeholder group does not mean that the justification is a persuasive or viable one. Indeed, those stakeholders against whose interests the manager has acted will certainly have reasons for doubting her justifications and she will be answerable to these groups as well. Hence, stakeholder groups will maintain managerial accountability in much the same way as described by James Madison in Federalist No. 10—various stakeholder "factions" will monitor management as well as one another.[17]

It would be interesting, though outside the scope of this chapter, to consider the implications of granting legal standing to some stakeholders in derivative lawsuits as a way of ensuring accountability. A derivative lawsuit is typically brought by a shareholder against an opportunistic manager or director *on behalf of the corporation*. If this legal right were extended (possibly one at a time beginning with employees) to other stakeholders, managerial accountability would be maintained, as would the agency relationship between managers (agents) and the corporation (principal) without great trauma to the existing legal framework. Such suits would not be brought on behalf of the stakeholders, however. The legal standing of stakeholders would be as representatives of the organization in which they have a stake.

Stakeholder theory cannot provide a specific objective function for the corporation.

Another common critique concerns the "radical under-determinism" of stakeholder theory; that is, "[i]n rejecting the maximisation of long-term owner value as the purpose of business, and requiring business instead simply to 'balance' the interests of all stakeholders, stakeholder theory discards the objective basis for evaluating business action"[18] and the theory therefore fails to be "illuminatingly action-guiding."[19]

In one sense, this critique is accurate: Stakeholder theory does fail to provide an algorithm for day-to-day managerial decision making, due to the level of abstraction at which the discussion is taking place. Stakeholder theory, as here elaborated and at the level of analysis addressed by the critique, provides a method by which stakeholder obligations are derived and an admonition that managers must account for the interests of these stakeholders when making decisions. It is impossible to say *a priori* what these interests will be and how they may be accounted for due to the myriad ways that an organization might be arranged (see Chapter 5 for a discussion of discourse ethics and the actual content of stakeholder obligations). This is among the criticisms leveled at moral and political theory as well as the motivation for the two-tiered approach to organizational ethics described in Chapter 3. It is impossible for such a theory to dictate specific action in the abstract.

However, this is another example of an evil genie criticism. The same critique may be leveled at the conventional shareholder-centered view. The managerial dictate to maximize shareholder wealth stands mute when queried, How? This is because of the innumerable ways to do so. Indeed, this indeterminacy and the impossibility of a one right way to manage is the reason for Donaldson and Dunfee's moral free space and the business judgment rule.

Ostensible critics of stakeholder theory, including Jensen and Sternberg, eagerly embrace an instrumental variation of stakeholder management as a means to "maximize the total market value of the firm" or "maximize long-term owner value," respectively. In his critique of stakeholder theory, Jensen concedes that "value maximizing says nothing about how to create a superior vision or strategy,"[20] though "[m]aximizing the total market value of the firm—that is the sum of the market values of the equity, debt and any other contingent claims outstanding on the firm—is one objective function that will resolve the tradeoff problem among multiple constituencies."[21] There is no reason to believe, however, that stakeholder management would be any easier or the theory more determinate when undertaken for instrumental rather than normative reasons. Moreover, instrumental stakeholder theory ignores the moral obligations described here. Stakeholder theory's critics frequently demand more of other theories than of their own.

Furthermore, the belief that maximizing "the total market value of the firm" or "long-term owner value" is more determinate than the balancing of stakeholder interests may itself prove dangerous due to what I term the delusion of determinacy. That is, under conditions of uncertainty and bounded rationality, managers may be led to believe that the standard objective function dictates action in a way that is more specific than stakeholder theory. It does not, and the belief that it does gives managers an unfounded sense of confidence in their decisions. Managerial wisdom and judgment are replaced with a false sense of mathematical precision.

After independently and collaboratively criticizing stakeholder theory for its ambiguity, longtime friendly critics of stakeholder theory Donaldson and Dunfee choose to conclude their book, *Ties That Bind*, with the following:

> As should be clear from the discussion above, an ISCT-based [integrative social contracts theory] stakeholder theory will not provide concrete external guidance for resolving every difficult question found in stakeholder management. *No theory or approach can, or even should, do that.* An internal revenue code level of detail in defining who is a stakeholder is neither possible nor desirable.[22]

As Donaldson and Dunfee indicate, it is important that scholars recognized the limitations of stakeholder theory—and shareholder theory, ISCT, and any other theory discussed at a similar level of abstraction. As demonstrated in later sections, many writers who are sympathetic to stakeholder theory have failed to recognize these limitations as well.

Finally, stakeholder theory, when applied to for-profit business organizations, is consistent with profit maximization. Let us distinguish, however, between profitability and *maximizing shareholder wealth* or *stock value/share price*. Maximizing profit says nothing about who gets a say in the decision making or who gets how much of this value, so maximized. It is only when the primary beneficiary of this profitability is constantly and exclusively a single stakeholder (e.g., equity share owners) that there is conflict between the theories. An organization that is managed for stakeholders will distribute the fruits of organizational success (and failure) among all legitimate stakeholders. Moreover, managing for stakeholders will include communication between managers and stakeholders concerning *how* profits should be maximized. Granting the imperative of profitability, there remain distributive and procedural issues to which stakeholder theory would draw attention. I turn now to an elaboration of this important distinction.

Stakeholder theory is primarily concerned with the distribution of financial outputs.

Debates regarding stakeholder theory frequently focus on how much each group gets (typically monetarily) from the organization; that is, who gets how much and why? However, also important is the matter of who is allowed to take part in decision making that concerns organizational objectives and strategies. At least since Freeman's work, *Strategic Management: A Stakeholder Approach,* the importance of procedural justice has been recognized. Who gets how much of the organizational outcomes pie is an important question, but so is who gets a say in how the pie is baked. Stakeholder theory is concerned with who has input in decision making as well as with who benefits from the outcomes of such decisions. Procedure is as important to stakeholder theory as distribution.

Social psychologists have long studied the distinction between distributive and procedural justice.[23] Not only have people been found to have an interest in the fairness of the final outcomes of a distributive process, but evidence also suggests that people are concerned about the justness of the process of distribution itself. Among the major findings of procedural justice research is that people are more accepting of outcomes when the procedure for distribution is perceived as fair—even in situations when the outcome itself is undesirable.[24] Hence, contrary to the suggestions of earlier work on distributive justice,[25] outcomes are not the only thing that matters in perceptions of justice. The fairness of the *procedures* employed is also determinative of fairness judgments.

Among the most important determinants of the fairness of a particular procedure is the degree of control within the process. That is, people find procedures that allow for greater participation in decision making to be fairer. As the perceived justice of outcomes is substantially determined by the perceived fairness of the process used in distribution, it follows that greater participation in decision making leads to an increase in the perceived fairness of the outcomes. Among the prescriptions of much of stakeholder theory is that relevant stakeholders should have input in the decision-making processes of the organization. This may be for either instrumental reasons (e.g., achieving "buy in") or normative reasons—the organization has a moral obligation to its stakeholders requiring that they have input into how the organization is run. Thus, stakeholder theorists and critics should be fully cognizant of the procedural prescriptions of the theory as well as the distributive.

Focus on *distribution* and a deemphasizing of *procedure* is not the only manner in which exclusive focus on distribution of outputs is a misinterpretation of stakeholder theory—*material* outputs are not the sole subject of distribution. Information is another vital good that is distributed among stakeholders by the organization. This non-zero-sum subject of distribution also plays a role in perceptions of fairness among stakeholders to the extent that full information contributes to the decision-making process among stakeholders. Transparency between the organization and its stakeholders contributes greatly to perceptions of fairness. Thus, to the extent that discussions of stakeholder theory frequently become preoccupied with the distribution of financial outputs, important issues of procedural fairness and the distribution of non-financial, informational goods are underemphasized; and stakeholder theory achieves significantly less than its full capacity.

Stakeholder management means that all stakeholders must be treated equally.

It is commonly asserted that stakeholder theory implies that all stakeholders must be treated equally irrespective of the fact that some obviously contribute more than others to the organization.[26] Prescriptions of equality have been inferred from discussions of "balancing" stakeholder interests and are in direct conflict with the advice of some experts on organizational design and reward systems.[27]

Marcoux is among those who make this criticism in his analysis of the concept of balance in stakeholder theory. He begins by outlining three potential interpretations of balance (or equity) on a stakeholder account:

Egalitarianism Distribution based on something like Rawls's difference principle (Rawls, 1971).[e]

Equalitarianism Equal shares for all stakeholders.

Pareto-Consequentialism Making at least one better without diminishing anyone.

Marcoux's arguments against these three candidates are largely sound; however, he misses one of the more obvious—and indeed strongest—interpretations of balance among organizational stakeholders: meritocracy.[f] On the most defensible conception of stakeholder theory, benefits are distributed based on relative contribution to the organization. The principle of stakeholder fairness emphasizes this conception with the equitable proportionality condition (see Chapter 5). This interpretation is also suggested in a quotation from the Sloan Colloquy.[28] They write: "Corporations should attempt to distribute the benefits of their activities as equitably as possible among stakeholders, *in light of their respective contributions, costs, and risks.*" Inasmuch as this quote was used early in Marcoux's paper to exemplify the centrality of balance to stakeholder theory, it is surprising that he fails to appeal to it in his own interpretations of balance.

---

[e]Rawls's difference principle says that social institutions should be arranged such that any inequalities in the distribution of social goods must redound to the benefit of the least well off.

[f]Paul Glezen has also suggested "balance" may be insightfully interpreted in the sense meant when discussing balance in wine. I do not pursue this interpretation, but merely point it out as an interesting variation.

Similarly, Sternberg argues that "in maintaining that all stakeholders are of equal importance to a business, and that business ought to be answerable equally to them all, stakeholder theory confounds business with government."[29] She cites no author, however, who argues for such equality of importance or managerial answerability. This is, again, suggestive of a straw-person argument. A meritocratic interpretation of stakeholder balance overcomes the objection that a stakeholder-based firm using either the egalitarian or equalitarian interpretation would be unable to obtain equity or any other manner of financing. Certainly financing is important to organizations and, as such, providers of this capital should garner a substantial portion of the economic benefits of the firm as well as receive a great deal of managerial attention in organizational decision making. On the conception of stakeholder theory proffered here, shareholders would get a fair return on their investment without managerial concern that is exclusive of other groups to whom an obligation is due.[g] Still less does the stakeholder theory confuse an organization with the state. As discussed later, the stakeholder theory described here is a theory of organizational strategy and ethics, not a theory of the whole political economy.

This meritocratic hierarchy is not the only criterion by which stakeholders may be arranged. In Chapter 6, I argue that stakeholders may usefully be separated into normative and derivative stakeholders. Normative stakeholders are those to whom the organization has a direct moral obligation to attend to their well-being. They provide the answer to the seminal stakeholder query, "For whose benefit ought the firm be managed?" Typically normative stakeholders are those most frequently cited in stakeholder discussions such as financiers, employees, customers, suppliers, and local communities.

---

[g]Notably, when profits are discussed among the visionary companies of Collins and Porras (1994), it is not in terms of maximization, but "*reasonable*" (Ford), "*fair*" (Johnson & Johnson), "*adequate*" (Motorola), and "*attractive*" (Marriott).

Alternatively, derivative stakeholders are those groups or individuals who can either harm or benefit the organization, but to whom the organization has no direct moral obligation as stakeholders.[h] This latter group might include such groups as competitors, activists, and the media.[i] The organization is not managed for the benefit of derivative stakeholders, but to the extent that they may influence the organization or its normative stakeholders, managers are obliged to account for them in their decision making. Far from strict equality, therefore, there are a number of more convincing ways that stakeholder theory may distinguish between and among constituency groups.

Social psychology may also contribute to the question of equality among stakeholders as well as the question of prioritizing among competing stakeholder claims. In a sense, this question underlies (is logically prior to) the question of procedural and distributive justice previously raised. The question of what proportion of the organizational outputs should go to a given stakeholder group or how much procedural input each constituency ought to have in a given decision presupposes agreement on the appropriate distributive scheme. Are all stakeholders equal (all deserving an equal proportion of organizational outputs and equal voice in decision making) or do some stakeholder groups deserve a greater proportion of the outputs and more consideration in decision making due to some notion of unequal input and merit?

Psychological studies of organizational justice have also considered the instrumental effects of different distributive values on the achievement of goals.[30] Leventhal and Deutsch have argued separately that differences in the method of distribution have instrumental effects on the relevant group

---

[h]The organization may have other duties or obligations to non-stakeholders, such as the duty to not cause harm to, lie to, or steal from them. These duties exist prior to and separate from stakeholder obligations and are not considered when establishing stakeholder status.

[i]These typical stakeholders are only for the purpose of generic example. Which specific groups are what sort of stakeholder, or indeed which are stakeholders at all, cannot be determined in the abstract. This can only be determined by reference to actual organizations in actual relationships with other groups.

within which the goods are distributed. Deutsch suggests the following hypotheses.

> In cooperative relations in which economic productivity is a primary goal, equity rather than equality or need will be the dominant principle of distributive justice. In cooperative relations in which the fostering or maintenance of enjoyable social relations is the common goal, equality will be the dominant principle of distributive justice.[31]

Similarly, Greenberg suggests the following:

> [P]eople believe that the maintenance of social harmony is promoted through the use of equal reward allocations, whereas the maximization of performance is promoted by systems that allocate outcomes equitably—that is, in proportion to relative performance (Deutsch, 1975, 1985).[32]

A number of studies bear out these hypotheses.[33]

Given these findings, the question of stakeholder prioritization depends—at least in part—upon the reasons and goals underlying the use of a stakeholder approach to management. If a stakeholder approach is employed to improve performance in the standard business senses, then equity is more appropriate as a distributive value. On the other hand, if greater harmony or a decrease in discord among stakeholders is the more important goal of the stakeholder approach, then equality as a basis for distribution better conduces to this goal. In the case of the for-profit organization, however, we expect that performance goals would be primary and thus equity will be the most commonly appropriate mode of distribution.

The method of stakeholder input is an open question. Everything from stakeholder representation on boards of directors to informal and nonspecific "concern" for stakeholders by decision makers has been suggested. However it is achieved, it is important for the sake of ethics, psychological well-being, and organizational success that stakeholders be accorded some say in determining not only how much of the organization's outputs they receive, but also how those outputs are created.

Friendly Misinterpretations

Many who would label themselves sympathetic to stakeholder theory have also contributed critical tinder to the project of razing stakeholder theory through overextension. I address a few such overextensions, and at least one case of unwarranted limitation, of stakeholder theory.

Stakeholder theory requires changes to current law.

Discussions of stakeholder theory have occasionally included calls for changes in the law. These changes may be either permissive or demanding. On the one hand, it might be argued that managing for stakeholders may be contrary to the legal requirement that managers maximize shareholder wealth. If it is the case that managing for stakeholders is illegal, the stakeholder theorist would argue the need for changes in the law so that it is at least *permissible* for managers to consider non-shareholders in their decision making. On the other hand, the stakeholder theorist might argue that the moral superiority of stakeholder theory demands legislation *requiring* managers to consider stakeholder interests in their decision making.

Regarding the legality of managing for stakeholders, Marens and Wicks[34] argue convincingly that the business judgment rule allows managers to manage for stakeholders as the law currently stands. Codifying their point is the explicit allowance in the statutes of the majority of states[35] that managers *may* consider stakeholders in their decision making. Most importantly for the purposes of this chapter, all of this may well be beside the point. Observation of practice and the concession of many stakeholder critics[36] suggests that managing for stakeholders is, in fact, the most effective way to run a business for *all* stakeholders, including shareholders. If this is the case, changes in the laws are superfluous.

A potentially controversial result of this point among business ethics and corporate social responsibility scholars is that stakeholder theory, as a managerial theory, does not require changing the structure of corporate governance.[37] The theory can reasonably remain agnostic, for example, concerning stakeholder representation on boards of directors. This does not rule out the possibility, or even advantage, of having stakeholder representation on boards. The requirement of such representation is, however, neither theoretically necessary nor intrinsic to stakeholder theory, per se. If stakeholder theory is interpreted as a theory of strategic management, then changes in law would be no more necessary than laws requiring organizations to be visionary,[38] excellent,[39] or learning.[40]

I recognize that the topic of stakeholder legislation may be the knottiest log I herein hew. Indeed, I briefly mention a potential legal change—legal standing for stakeholders in corporate derivative suits—in an earlier section of this chapter. As a managerial theory, with at least some roots in classical liberalism (i.e., libertarianism[41]), stakeholder theory is neither legally prohibited nor in need of permissive or demanding legislation and regulation. In short, discourse concerning the legal relationship between the organization and its stakeholders is welcome, but the theory does not require a change in the law to remain viable.

Stakeholder theory is thinly veiled socialism and refers to the entire economy.

Though a popular subject for discussion in the United Kingdom and Europe, the "stakeholder economy" is not the more humble variation of stakeholder theory advocated here.

Stakeholder theory (as I understand it) is a theory of organizational strategy and ethics and not a theory of political economy. *Stakeholder* is not synonymous with *citizen* or *moral agent*, as some wish to interpret it. Rather, a particular and much closer relationship between an organization and a constituency group is required for stakeholder status. The theory is delimited and non-stakeholder should remain a meaningful category.

Some commentators and politicians argue for an interpretation of stakeholder theory in a broad sociopolitical context. Perhaps most famous among these interpretations is a 1996 speech by then British Labour Party leader Tony Blair, entitled "The Stakeholder Economy," which continues to receive a great deal of attention both in favor and in opposition. Supporters of this concept suggest that although stakeholder theory was originally applied to the private sector, they believe expanding stakeholder theory to include public institutions is a conceptual advance.[42] While the effort to take organizations seriously in political theory should be applauded, this particular translation from organization theory to political theory represents an unwarranted dilution of stakeholder theory. Further, this watering down makes stakeholder theory more susceptible to charges that it is overly broad and hollow; or, if meaningful, the stakeholder economy amounts to little more than the "new socialism"—its contribution to the stakeholder debate being the sparse and occasional insertion of the word *stakeholder* into a tract about leftist macroeconomic policy.[43]

Perraton[44] exemplifies the dilution of stakeholder theory in arguing that "there needs to be frameworks for constructing stakeholder arrangements not just at the local and national levels, but also at the regional and global levels." Arguments adduced for this position are:

> first, that globalisation has undermined the relations within a national economy that the concept of a stakeholder economy was based upon, and second that agents are now enmeshed in a

range of relationships that extend beyond national boundaries. Although this implies that the project of constructing a national stakeholders economy is no longer tenable, it does not necessarily mean that the idea of stakeholding has become obsolete.[45]

Quite so. I maintain that these same conditions imply a greater need for *organizational-level* policies and individual responsibility and recognition of stakeholder obligations rather than supernational laws, taxes, and regulations. When everyone in the world is a stakeholder of everyone else, the term adds little if any value and the critics' charge of conceptual emptiness becomes a rather convincing one.

The justification of stakeholder-based social policy is frequently couched in terms of the need for legislation/regulation to *permit* the stakeholder economy to flourish.[46] These discussions often proceed to describe a stakeholder economy in which the stakeholder model is *enforced* by the state. This is an important distinction. The several state-level "other constituency statutes" in the United States (probably unnecessarily) render stakeholder organizations *permissible* under the law, but only one state requires consideration of other stakeholders. A managerial (or libertarian) stakeholder theory would fully assent to permissive stakeholder legislation (or the alteration of laws that preclude stakeholder organizations), but the version advanced by advocates of a stakeholder society would attempt to enforce, by fiat of state, stakeholder management. If managing for stakeholders is a superior method for running most organizations, enforcement is inefficient and superfluous.

Another significant point of departure between managerial stakeholder theory and the stakeholder society is the relationship between benefits (rights) and obligations. For advocates of the stakeholder society, "the benefits of stakeholding for the individual stakeholder are contingent on the carrying out of associated obligations."[47] Kelly, Kelly, and Gamble suggest similarly that "much stricter obligations are being enforced on the recipient to find work or undertake train-ing."[48] For a managerial stakeholder theory, this gets the con-tingency backwards—obligations arise from the voluntary activities of individuals and organizations. On the justification of stakeholder obligations elaborated here, it is precisely the acceptance of benefits that creates obligations rather than the benefits being contingent upon carrying out obligations. Of course, the continued provision of benefits requires the fulfill-ment of obligations among stakeholders on both accounts, as stakeholder relationships are reciprocal. The difference lies in how obligations are originally generated among individuals and organizations. On the stakeholder society account, obli-gations and the associated benefits simply exist among people. As here conceived, stakeholder obligations require some vol-untary action and, in contrast to duties, exist between discrete entities rather than as a diffuse, all-inclusive concept.

Stakeholder theory is a comprehensive moral doctrine.

In his discussion of the idea of an overlapping consensus, Rawls distinguishes between his own theory and what he terms "comprehensive moral doctrines". A comprehensive moral doctrine is one that is able to cover the entirety of the moral universe without reference to any other competing theory. All moral questions can be answered from within a comprehen-sive moral doctrine. Rawls claims that not only does his con-ception not depend on a single religious, national, cultural, or moral theory for its foundation, but also that it is consistent with a "reasonable pluralism" of such doctrines. One need not convert from her preferred doctrine to accept justice as fair-ness. All reasonable moral doctrines already accept it from within their own conception.

Moreover, not only is stakeholder theory not a compre-hensive moral doctrine, but also is yet another step removed even from Rawls's own theory. Stakeholder theory is a theory of organizational ethics. As described in Chapter 3, theories of organizational ethics are distinct from moral and political theories due to the difference in the subject matter of the various disciplines.[49] Contrary to the assumptions of political theory, organizations are, according to Rawls, voluntary associations rather than a part of the basic structure of society. Further, interaction within and between organizations creates moral obligations over and above those duties that arise due simply to one's status as a human being or citizen of a nation.

Stakeholder theory is not intended to provide an answer to all moral questions. Stakeholder-based obligations do not even take precedence in all moral questions in an organizational context. Violations of the human rights of a constituency group by commercial organizations and the gratuitous destruction of the natural environment are morally wrong, but such judgments rely on concepts outside of stakeholder theory as herein delimited.[50] Stakeholder theory shares this delimitation with its supposed rival theory of shareholder wealth maximization—at least as elaborated by Friedman. Friedman's defense of shareholder wealth maximization is a moral one based on the property rights of shareholders. Noteworthy for my purposes, Friedman's admonition includes the condition that shareholder wealth maximization must take place within the constraints of law and morality. This suggests another level of analysis operative in Friedman's system. So too is the case with stakeholder theory.

Consider, for example, Donaldson and Dunfee's suggestion:

> All organizations, wherever situated, and whatever their characteristics, must recognize the interests of stakeholders whenever failing to do so may violate a hypernorm . . . it then becomes the obligation of all organizations to recognize this principle in regard to stakeholders. Thus, as DeGeorge suggests, an organization that sells carcinogen-contaminated pajamas in the Third World, knowing that they are prohibited for sale in the United

States and Europe and are unacceptably dangerous to the intended users, fails to recognize a mandatory stakeholder duty.[51]

A hypernorm, according to Donaldson and Dunfee, indicates a duty that applies to all organizations and individuals irrespective of their context. Though clearly an important moral idea, violation of a hypernorm lies outside the scope of stakeholder theory as a managerial theory of organizational ethics. The action described is a violation of human rights irrespective of the stakeholder status (or lack thereof) of the customer. Though it may be a violation of a stakeholder obligation, this violation is secondary to the hypernorm violation. Stakeholder theory adds as much to the question of selling unacceptably dangerous, carcinogen-contaminated pajamas as the principle of truth-telling adds to the question of lying to a person you have just stabbed in the chest. There are issues morally prior to stakeholder obligations and truth-telling in play in these cases.

This delimitation on stakeholder theory is not important only in cases of negative injunction such as violations of human rights. Stakeholder theory, as a theory of the obligatory, also contributes little to the question of corporate philanthropy and supererogation in general. There will always be actions that organizations *may* take but that are not obligatory from a stakeholder perspective. Such activities are what Carroll[52] refers to as "Voluntary/Discretionary" and Donaldson and Dunfee call "moral free space," and are neither prohibited nor required by stakeholder theory.

Orts writes:

Corporations have had a long-standing right to give away a portion of their earnings to philanthropic organizations chosen by management. It is not easy to see how this recognised right of gift-giving by business firms fits with stakeholder theory. The best response of stakeholder theory would be to expand the definition of stakeholder to include society as a whole, but at this point

the theory begins to lose its shape. If the entire society is a stakeholder, then how can any decision be made on the basis of comparing different stakeholders within a business?[53]

But, as indicated, this "best response" is not one shared by the
present authors for the same reasons that Orts provides (i.e.,
the problem of stakeholder identity). However, philanthropy
would not and need not be justified by reference to a theory
of the obligatory such as stakeholder theory. Rather, charitable
giving stands above and outside of a description of what is
required of organizations. A comprehensive moral doctrine
would (perhaps) be expected to address duties of charity.
Stakeholder theory need not.

Stakeholder theory applies only to corporations.

Whereas the preceding friendly misinterpretations tend
toward overextension of the theory, I would argue that this
final misinterpretation represents an unnecessary limitation
on the scope of stakeholder theory. Though not always the
case (the SRI definition uses "organizations" as their subject
domain), the word *stakeholder* has come to focus primarily on
the publicly owned corporation. Indeed, in the most commonly quoted work of stakeholder theory since Freeman, Donaldson and Preston write:

> [A] normative [stakeholder] theory attempts to interpret the
> function of, and offer guidance about, the *investor-owned corpora-
> tion* on the basis of some underlying moral or philosophical
> principles.[54]

This focus is only intensified by the tendency of management
scholars more generally to concentrate on large, multinational
corporations as the objects of their research. This has led to a
disproportionate, nearly exclusive attention on the part of
stakeholder theorists within business schools on the corporation. Less attention has been paid to stakeholder theory in the

context of other organizational forms such as small or family owned businesses, privately owned concerns of any size, partnerships, nonprofits, and governmental organizations. This may appear appropriate if stakeholder theory's primary role is its opposition to the shareholder wealth maximization view. However, for stakeholder theory to truly come into its own as a theory of strategic management and organizational ethics, it will need to be applied to more than just the large, publicly held corporation.

Conclusion

This chapter attempts to add clarity to stakeholder theory by addressing a number of straw-person objections posed by critics of the theory as well as a few friendly overextensions and distortions averred by stakeholder theory advocates. I do not presume to dictate the research agenda of other scholars; however, it is important to avoid talking past the many intelligent and thoughtful opponents of stakeholder theory and to avoid "preaching to choir" by offering extensions that will only convince one who already advocates some version of the theory. By clearing away some of the most common misconceptions of stakeholder theory, we are in a better position to see both the power and the limitations of this approach.

CHAPTER 3

Why *Organizational* Ethics?[55]

*The fault of methodological hierarchies is not unlike the
fault of political and social ones: they lead to a distortion of
vision with a consequent misdirection of effort.*

—JOHN RAWLS[56]

*The reasons Aristotle gave for saying that politics is the cul-
mination of ethics are today reasons for saying that business
ethics is the culmination of ethics.*

—EDWIN HARTMAN[57]

Organizations need an ethics of their own, distinct from
both political theory and moral philosophy.[a] I am not
the first to discern something distinctive about organizations,
something that calls for a distinct moral framework.[58] However, theories that have propelled organizational ethics to the

---

[a]By "distinct" I mean something less severe than many people's interpretation. I use distinctions as a means of clarifying, with no implication of mutual exclusivity or collective
exhaustiveness. As should become clear in the chapter, I am not arguing for a complete separation of organizational ethics from moral and political theory. Rather, a greater sensitivity
to the distinctive features of organizations should make for a more discerning and practical
organization-level moral theory.

point of seeing this need are ironically ill suited to address it. The full implications of taking organizations seriously have not been drawn, because the distinctions between organizations and states and between organizations and individuals have not been drawn sharply enough. To move beyond a dawning recognition of these differences, I flesh them out and indicate how they reorient organizational ethics, setting it upon its own footing.

Why a Theory of *Organizational* Ethics?

Organizations differ from individuals and from states in important ways. The ethical theory constructed to guide each should therefore differ in important ways. Classical political theory and individual moral theory are inadequate for dealing with the moral problems that arise in the context of the modern corporation. More fundamental, though, than the substantive differences between persons, states, and organizations are the implications for *constructing* an ethics of organizations. To develop organizational ethics requires an understanding of the inadequacies of moral and political theory. Those inadequacies do more than limit the application of moral and political theory to organizations. They point up the need to approach the development of organizational ethics differently.

In form, organizations differ from states and individuals in morally relevant ways much the way states differ from individuals. Considerations arise on the part of the government and the governed concerning the special obligations and duties of citizenship that are in addition to those duties owed to one another as *humans* (i.e., those duties suggested by much of moral philosophy). Examples of such additional considerations include the legitimacy of the use of coercion with regard to citizens, duties to pay taxes, and the performance of other civic duties (e.g., military service). This is not to say that moral philosophy is unimportant in the political sphere. People retain nearly all of the duties, rights, and liberties they had as *humans* when considered as *citizens*. However, a new set of duties and obligations is *added* by one's role as citizen or government official.

A parallel situation exists vis-à-vis the organization. The duties and liberties one has as a human being, as well as the duties, liberties, and obligations one has as a citizen, are still extant. However, economic engagement and interaction, and organizational life, create yet another set of obligations between the person and that particular economic cooperative scheme. The argument of this chapter is that, like the differences between moral and political philosophy that justify an interesting distinction between the two, there exist interesting differences between both of these spheres and the sphere of the organization. The aim, then, is to illuminate the need for and implications of a separate study of organizational ethics.

Leading theorists have already grasped the fundamental importance of organizations, at least on a substantive level. Business ethicists have already begun examining substantive questions regarding how such entities ought to be governed. As part of an ongoing colloquy with economists, ethicists map out their own models of the firm and its origins. Whether construed as contracts[59] or communities,[60] mediating institutions,[61] or commons,[62] organizations have begun to captivate the attention of ethicists. In developing these theories, however, business ethics as a field has only partially grasped the significance of organizations.

The goals of this chapter are twofold: first, to outline why political theory and moral philosophy prove inadequate for organizations; second, to indicate how these inadequacies illuminate the distinctive issues and problems confronting organizational ethics, as well as the options distinctively available to it.

In light of the role organizations now play in society, and in light of the influence they exercise over individuals' conduct, organizations warrant philosophers' attention. The ethics that govern organizations cannot, however, be mere derivations or applications of political or moral theory. Among others, Freeman,[63] Hartman,[64] and Donaldson and Dunfee[65] provide compelling arguments for organizational ethics. Although their theories move some distance toward a distinct organization ethics, they are hamstrung by their own methods, for they proffer theories heavily (perhaps exceedingly) dependent upon classical politico-moral theory.

Limitations of Political Theory for Organizations

Political theory is concerned with the proper arrangement of the state, in accord with justifiable ordering principles. The question of how society should be governed, and on what basis an initial arrangement might be justified, has been revived with great vigor by John Rawls.[66] His *A Theory of Justice* has influenced more than just political philosophy, however. His concepts of the original position, the veil of ignorance, and the difference principle have found a role in business ethics[67] even though Rawls explicitly confines the bulk of his theory to the "basic structure" of society and its "major social institutions." The basic structure provides the foundation upon which the various other associations and communities, including businesses, operate. The political constitution, the legally recognized forms of property, the organization of the economy, and the nature of the family belong to the basic structure. In contrast, business and other private organizations are part of what Rawls calls the "'background culture' of civil society . . . the culture of the social, not of the political . . . the culture of daily life."[68]

To understand the inadequacy of political theory for organizational ethics, consider Rawls's distinction between a

"well-ordered society" and "communities and associations."[b]
The agreements that establish the basic structure, and the
principles that govern it, differ markedly from the agreements pertaining to these other collectives (communities
and associations). Although it is tempting to apply Rawlsian
methods (e.g., the original position, the veil of ignorance[c])
in constructing organizational ethics, applying those mechanisms and principles is misplaced for both methodological
and substantive reasons.

From a methodological perspective, the *process* of constructing a just basic structure (e.g., from behind the veil of
ignorance) is designed for the basic structure, nothing else.[69]
Rawls—indeed political theory in general—is concerned with
establishing the background rules and institutions that will govern all of civil society. The ethics of associations and civil society within a Rawlsian framework assume a just basic structure.
So applying to organizations the mechanisms and principles
used to create a just basic structure is tantamount to designing
traffic laws in accord with the laws of human flight. If we could
indeed fly, then the natural laws and structures permitting such
flight would create a reality so far different from the one we
now experience that intelligible viable, and relevant traffic laws

---

[b]By no means do I mean to suggest either that Rawls' is the only theory of political/moral
philosophy available. I have chosen to focus on Rawls's theory because: (1) his theory makes
and thereby allows for a version of the distinction I wish to defend here, (2) his theory is
explicit about the differences between organizations and civil society making the handles
easier to grasp, (3) he defended a similar conceptual distinction between moral and political theory (Rawls, 1975, 1999), (4) his work is among the most widely cited by all ethicists,
and therefore by organizational ethicists, and (5) this usage of Rawls's work in organizational contexts is frequently misused in the ways I elaborate. I readily acknowledge that
other theories deal with the issues I raise in different, more and less convincing, ways. My
thanks to John Rowan and Ed Hartman (2001) for suggesting this clarification.

[c]The veil of ignorance and original position refer to the thought experiment Rawls uses to
model fairness in the creation of a social contract to govern the basic structure of society.
He argues that only if we abstract away from our contingent inequalities will the resulting
agreement be truly fair. Thus, behind the veil of ignorance and in the original position, the
decision makers do not know their place in society, family background, talent, intelligence,
work ethic, or other distinguishing characteristics. From behind this veil of ignorance, people can arrive at an equitable arrangement of society's benefits and burdens that will be fair
to all because they did not know who they will be when the veil is lifted and society goes
about its activity. They will have no incentive to create a society that privileges their own
group because they do not know to which group they will belong.

would need to be far different from anything we could now imagine. How organizations are to be arranged depends upon the way the basic structure is arranged. If the basic structure were "well ordered," then organizations would be far different from those we have. Since the basic structure is not in fact "well ordered," organizations must be arranged in such a way that takes its imperfections into account.

It may nonetheless be reasonable to ask how Rawlsian methods help to imagine how organizations might be arranged. Perhaps we cannot fathom how organizations might ideally be arranged within a "well-ordered society," but, the argument might go, even if the veil of ignorance, original position, and difference principle are intended for the basic structure, might we still gain insight and guidance from considering organizations in their light? The answer lies in the substantive differences distinguishing organizations from states.

The devices used to imagine an ideal basic structure function to handle the unique problems of political philosophy. Rawlsian methods are designed to establish a just basic structure, and that structure and its undergirding agreements are coercive and involuntary in ways that associations are not, just as associations are teleological in ways that the basic structure is not. These differences indicate how political philosophy and the problems it must address are markedly incongruous with organizational ethics and the problems it must address. Consider three substantive differences between states and organizations: freedom of exit, value of contribution, and orienting aims and purposes.

Freedom of Exit   One may not appeal to the right to exit in establishing the background rules of the basic structure, according to Rawls.[d] That is, "[w]hile the principles adopted

---

[d]Rawls's "strains of commitment" argument for the "maximin" criterion relies importantly on the inability to exit from the state that is to be ordered according to the (rationally) chosen principles of justice.

will no doubt allow for emigration (subject to suitable qualifications), they will not permit arrangements that would be just only if emigration were allowed."[70] In this way the initial hypothetical agreement in the original position and the system of social cooperation that it creates is quite different from the subsequent agreements that characterize private associations and communities. While seeking morally appropriate norms for most private associations, it is perfectly acceptable to consider exit as a viable alternative. That is what qualifies them as voluntary associations.

While I do not wist to suggest that anything like *perfect* freedom of exit exists in organizations,[e] the possibility of exit is constitutive of organizational membership, just as its impossibility is constitutive of societal membership. In fact, organizational ethics must explain the moral implications of deviations from this freedom of exit—asymmetric freedom, for example, or freedom short of that necessary to constitute volition. Such an issue so central to organizations is not even a possibility in Rawlsian political theory. Exit from organizations is not methodologically ruled out as it is for Rawls.

Notably, the possibility of optional entry and exit provided the main point of distinction between "justice" and "fairness" in Rawls's early work:

> Justice and fairness are, indeed, different concepts, but they share a fundamental element in common, which I shall call the concept of reciprocity. They represent this concept as applied to two distinct cases: very roughly, justice to a practice in which there is no option whether to engage in it or not, and one must play; fairness to a practice in which there is such an option, and one may decline the invitation.[71]

---

[e]One danger of applying political theory to organizations lies in our tendency to caricature the possibility of exit. Either it is overestimated or considered non-problematic; rarely is it accurately assessed. An organizational ethics that is sensitive to the level of freedom of exit actually available to people in organizations—due to differences in class, gender, nationality, geography, education, income and so on—would better model the moral obligations and duties within these myriad collectives.

This is consistent with the emphasis on reciprocity and private associations in the principle of stakeholder fairness elaborated upon in a later chapter.

Another related difference between the basic structure and private associations is the possibility of ejection of one or several members by other members. For reasons related to the distinctions that will be elaborated, organizations may occasionally have cause to withdraw an individual's membership in the group. Although rarely an issue for political theory, ejection of members from private associations is commonplace. Some might say all too commonplace, but the need for that very discussion points to the importance of the distinction. Exit for Rawls refers to a decision made by the exiting individual, but equally important are exits resulting from the decisions of others. Exit is either rarely considered in political theory or ruled out entirely.

Also related to this distinction is the fact that the basic structure institutions are generally considered to have a monopoly on the legitimate use of force. Basic structure institutions may physically compel compliance with its mandates in a way that private associations may not.

Value of Contribution Another difference between the agreements that form the basic structure and those that constitute associations is the knowledge and control one has over one's commitment and contribution. In the case of the initial agreement, we cannot know what we (or society) would be like in our absence. This idea is represented in the original position through exclusion of knowledge of contingent natural and social facts about the person as well as the state of the society in which one is to live. In contrast, our contributions to an association, and the association's contribution to us, are important determinants of whether we choose to join, are invited to join, and choose to remain part of a particular association or cooperative venture. Such considerations are irrelevant to the initial political agreement. Membership in civil society is taken as fixed.

At the level of private associations, it is acceptable for both individual members and organizations to have knowledge of the relative contribution of the other prior to a decision to interact. This is seen in the greater acceptability of meritocratic arrangements within organizations as compared with the basic structure. In political philosophy, and hence from the perspective of the nation-state, persons are conceived of as free and *equal.* This is not necessarily true to the same extent from the perspective of organizations. Social psychologists distinguish between equality, whereby each individual gets an equal amount, and equity, whereby each individual is rewarded based on relative contribution or some other (not necessarily equal) criterion.[72]

Meritocracy is not without its ethical problems[73] and the criteria upon which organization members are in fact rewarded may differ from publicly espoused criteria, and both may diverge from ethically justifiable grounds. Nonetheless, the underlying sense that organizations (unlike states) may justifiably distribute benefits (jobs, compensation, incentives, decision-making input) in a way that takes account of a person's contributions remains valid. Similarly, employees (unlike citizens) may choose to join or contribute to an organization in light of the organization's mission. Because organizations have purposes and aims, they will select and reward those people based on their capacity to contribute to the organization's purposes and aims. So too will employees choose to join organizations in light of the purposes and aims to which they wish to contribute.

Ends and Aims   There are no ends of a well-ordered society in the way that there are for other associations. People join and remain with associations, just as they are recruited and evaluated, on the basis of the associations' objectives. In contrast, the state should be neutral in its preference for any particular set of values, other than those that permit individual liberty in choosing a conception of the good and living by it. We may well want to prevent the state from underwriting and promoting particular objectives, but within realms of activity, such as business or the professions, we have equal reason to propose and debate the good that people engaged in those activities should be pursuing. Where aims may be anathema to the units of political philosophy—states—they seem equivalently vital to the units of organizational ethics.

In sum, freedom and possibility of exit, the mutual evaluation of contributions, and the presence of aims indicate that organizations are not equivalent to states. Organizations differ from states in characteristics considered constitutive of each entity. The approaches devised to construct ethical guidelines for the political and organizational spheres must thus reflect each sphere's particular characteristics.

To demonstrate some of the problems that arise when political philosophy is adapted to the needs of organizational ethics, consider the use of Rawls's "original position" at the level of the organization. His original position and veil of ignorance are thought experiments used to model equality in the social contract. From the perspective of liberal democracy, all persons should be treated as equals. Nowhere is this more important than in the establishment of major political institutions—the goal of the social contract. Rawls argues that inequalities are morally arbitrary. Differences such as race, religion, ethnicity, intelligence, talents, and even work ethic are the result of the "natural lottery" and should therefore not be considered in creating the basic structure of social institutions. When arguing from the original position, one must abstract away such distinctions. By this procedure, individuals will be unable to favor themselves or their class, because they do not know to which class they will belong once the veil of ignorance is lifted and fairness is thereby assured. Rawls explicitly argues that such equality only applies at the level or the nation-state and not at the level of private associations. The latter are the concern of organizational ethics.

Notwithstanding Rawls's own resistance, Edwin Hartman argues that we "need not be so reluctant to apply his [original position] device to organizations."[74] The suggestion is plausible: The differences between the basic structure and private associations are a matter of degree, with the largest and most powerful economic organizations exhibiting many of the characteristics of basic-structure institutions. This does not necessarily imply, however, that the differences are inconsequential.

Rawls's "original position" derives its power in part from the stipulation that—in accord with "thin" principles of a whole society or nation-state (i.e., human rights, "hypernorms", etc.)—persons are equal. Indeed, Sandel has argued persuasively that there may just as well be only one person behind a Rawlsian veil of ignorance since all are assumed identical for its purposes.[75] Hence, no relevantly similar person should be treated differently by the state *qua citizen*. Civil society is not a meritocracy: The liberal ideal is that of equality, and equality makes an original position thought experiment a *relatively* simple one at the level of the nation-state.[f]

However, an organization's stakeholders are not equal in this radical sense. Some contribute more to an organization's specific goals and thus have "legitimate expectations" (to use Rawls's terminology) to a greater portion of the benefits of organizational efforts. This inequality renders an organizational original position argument exponentially

---

[f]This is not meant to indicate that it is overly simple nor is it to take anything away from Rawls's monumental accomplishment. Rather liberal equality vis-à-vis the state and civil society renders the original position at least manageable in a way that it would not be in the case of organizations.

more complex. Such an original position would have to stipulate, at least, the following:

- The goal of the group (a matter that is prone to change)
- Who is to be included in the original position deliberations (a matter even more prone to change)[g]
- What is to be counted as contributing to that goal
- What sorts of psychological attributes are to be assumed of the "founders"

This list of complications merely scratches the surface of probable complications of an organizational original position. There are reams of criticism of Rawls's original position,[76] and he had to deal with only a fraction of what would be demanded of an organizational original position. To advocate the original position for organizational theorizing is to underestimate the complexity created by the specific goals organizations have, in contrast to the state, which thus allow (perhaps demand) more specific moral norms.

Also, Rawls employs what he calls a "thin theory of the good" as a sort of bootstrap argument. He needs this "thin

---

[g]R. Edward Freeman (1994 and personal correspondence) has suggested that the idea of organizational stakeholders is analytic to the concept of business. As such, he stipulates the five primary stakeholders (financiers, customers, suppliers, employees, and communities) as the relevant parties to his own veil of ignorance argument without addressing the subject of stakeholder identity and is thus able to circumvent the problem of stakeholder identification.

His treatment retains, however, the notion of equality as characterizing stakeholder relationships rather than equity as the current project advocates. Freeman writes:

> The normative core for this redesigned contractual theory will capture the liberal idea of fairness if it ensures a basic equality among stakeholders in terms of their moral rights as these are realized in the firm, and if it recognizes that inequalities among stakeholders are justified if they raise the level of the least well off stakeholder. (Freeman, 1994, pp. 515f)

The difference between Freeman's conception and the one advocated here is demonstrated by his employment of the "difference principle" *within organizations*. The current project suggests a distinction between citizenship and organizational membership (a distinction that Freeman believes to be incorrect). It is at the level of the basic structure where the difference principle does its work due to the liberal notion of equality among citizens. Our argument is that such equality does not obtain to the same degree within organizations and, hence, the difference principle does not apply intraorganizationally or among stakeholders. The difference principle is appropriate among groups characterized primarily by equality, but is less appropriate within the individual organizations where equity obtains.

theory" to get his argument off the ground. He argues that certain "primary goods" will be beneficial to any plan of life those in the original position may have in the actual world.[h] Agreement on the list of primary goods is a prerequisite for agreement in Rawls's original position.

The problem for organizational ethics theorists is that the list of goods necessary for the achievement of the myriad possible organizational goals—the necessity of which was discussed in the previous section—will be not only different for each organization but also a much longer list than the list of primary goods Rawls invokes. The theory of the good that would have to be employed by Hartman's founders would, necessarily, be much "thicker"[77] than that allowed for by original position arguments. Further, the theory of the good must be agreeable to all parties in the original position before selection from the list of alternatives can begin. As the theory of the good grows thicker, such agreement is less likely. The thicker theory of the good is a direct result of greater goal specificity at the organizational level. In other words, as the goals of a collective become more specific (as we move from the level of the basic structure to the level of private associations), the concomitant theory of the good must become thicker and hence more contentious and less amenable to agreement.

This brings up another problem for an organizational original position. Rawls's contractors are choosing from among a limited list of alternative principles in the original position. That is, the list of alternatives must not only be finite but also short enough to make comparisons between them possible. Hartman's founders will almost certainly run afoul of this condition. Organizations admit of myriad variations. Certainly there are more acceptable ways of morally arranging a given organization than there are morally acceptable ways of arranging a nation-state. As such, the list of possible,

---

[h]For Rawls, the primary goods are "liberty and opportunity, income and wealth, and the bases of self-respect." See Rawls, 1971, p. 62.

morally acceptable organizational forms would be far too large and unwieldy to admit of comparison within the original position. The original position contractors run headlong into Donaldson and Dunfee's problem of bounded moral rationality and the need for moral free space.[78]

Finally, the original position was designed to model the equality of citizens from the state's point of view. Such equality is the liberal ideal for the case of citizens, and Rawls's veil of ignorance captures this ideal in a vivid and useful way. However, the matter at hand is the extent to which organizations are characterized by this kind of equality or whether the notion of meritocratic "equity" is a better description of the distributive criterion within organizations (both descriptively and normatively). The liberal state is not a meritocracy, and hence equality of the kind modeled by the original position is appropriate in determining the shape of the basic structure. Organizations on the other hand may be described as meritocratic. While the original position methodology portrays equality well, it has a great deal more difficulty modeling considerations of equity. See Chapter 2 for a discussion of equity and equality in stakeholder theory.

Limitations of Moral Philosophy for Organizations

The preceding has demonstrated the problems that can arise when adapting political philosophy to organizational uses. Similar difficulties arise in the direct application of the classics of moral philosophy to organizational moral issues.[i] In laying the groundwork for their Integrative Social Contracts Theory (ISCT), Donaldson and Dunfee vividly describe one of the major inadequacies of moral theory in an organizational context.[79]

---

[i]Similarly to an earlier footnote in the context of Rawls's political theory, I readily concede that our criticisms here do not apply equally to all moral theories and to some not at all. The points do apply sufficiently to serve as examples of the conceptual dangers associated with the direct application of moral philosophy to organizational ethics.

They delineate between the macrosocial and microsocial contracts. Macrosocial contracts are those that apply between and within all organizations and persons in civil society—they establish the universal norms and duties. Microsocial contracts are those more specific and particular norms and duties that apply to individual organizations under the umbrella of the macrosocial contract.

Important for current purposes is the reasoning behind making this distinction. The macrosocial contract is necessary for two reasons. The first is to provide society with a backdrop of moral rules (or set of "thin" guidelines) that apply to all by virtue of their humanity or citizenship.[80] More interesting for current purposes is the macro justification of the micro sphere. Donaldson and Dunfee find the moral minimum social guidelines as insufficient for guiding behavior in cases where people are called upon to work more closely toward a common goal: "Both general moral theories and stakeholder theory seem incapable of expressing the moral complexity necessary to provide practical normative guidance for many business ethics contexts."[81] In these latter cases, "thicker" conceptions are needed; we need the microsocial norms. The macro-micro distinction exists because the original social contractors would have insisted upon it on Donaldson and Dunfee's account due to the "bounded moral rationality" of the macrosocial contractors.

Bounded moral rationality is among the most ingenious features of ISCT and provides a vivid way of redescribing the subject matter of this chapter. Bounded moral rationality refers to two primary forms of limitation:

1. Limits on the ability of general moral theory to model the full range of accepted moral convictions
2. Limits on the conceptual ability of individual moral agents to discover and process morally relevant facts[82]

The concept of bounded moral rationality models first the fact that the general moral theories of the past are inadequate for guiding behavior at the necessary level of specificity of daily life on Donaldson and Dunfee's account. For example, the requirement that one should act so as to maximize utility tells one little about the actions a manager ought to take regarding the environmental activists that have chained themselves to the gate of your facility demanding that the production process be made less harmful to the natural environment. Nor is much concrete assistance provided by the admonition that the manager act so that her actions are universalizable and that people are treated as ends and not as mere means. Does the manager have any additional moral obligations to the activists that should be considered in the decision? How about the local community? Does the natural environment itself have any moral standing and, if so, what is the nature of that standing? None of these problems seems amenable to being answered using only the general principles of moral and political theory. Though general moral theories may inform the decision, another level of moral consideration is necessary in the more specific context.

Further, even if someone were to come up with the "True" moral theory that is able to model all of the vagaries and apparent inconsistencies of moral life, such a theory would be unmanageable by most human beings given our limited time and cognitive capacity. This is the idea of item 2 in the previous list and is the more standard notion of bounded rationality from economics and organization theory.[83]

Being aware of the problems of bounded moral rationality, the macrosocial contractors would agree to leave a degree of "moral free space" within which to interact at the micro level.[j] In this way the bounded moral rationality of the

---

[j]The idea of "moral free space" should not be confused with Gauthier's notion of a "morally free zone." See David Gauthier, 1986, *Morals by Agreement* (New York: Oxford University Press). Donaldson and Dunfee are discussing the existence of a degree of flexibility at the level of private associations, whereas Gauthier intends that, under certain conditions, there may exist a sphere of human interaction that need not be concerned with matters of ethics and justice. It is clear that Donaldson and Dunfee do not have in mind a zone where ethics have no place, but rather a zone where the specific actors may exercise some discretion in the establishment of moral norms.

macrosocial contractors justifies the existence of microsocial contracts. These microsocial contracts, then, provide the thick norms that are required to conduct business at the level of private associations and the two-tiered social contract methodology is justified.

Although there exist justifiable reservations with regard to the social contract methodology, the arguments for bounded moral rationality are persuasive. Classical moral theory does not sufficiently account for the bounded moral rationality of its subjects. This is still another reason behind the call for an ethics of organizations.

Toward an Ethics of Organizations

It is somewhat easier to decry the limitations of existing approaches to organizational ethics, to descry the need for alternatives, and even to suggest criteria for developing alternatives, than it is to formulate fundamentally new approaches. As an initial, exploratory effort, however, the following characteristics are suggested as essential to an ethics of organizations.

Substantive Aims   To this point the idea of organizational aims has been used in a descriptive manner. Specific aims and purposes were among the important characteristics of organizations that rendered traditional moral and political theory inadequate, creating the need for a specifically organizational ethical model. Here the idea of aims is used in a more prescriptive way.

Ethical aims provide one avenue for keeping ethics alive and influencing everyday conduct. Aims determine what people see as the features of a situation demanding action. Aims enable agents to construct, evaluate, and revise their views of a problematic situation.[84] Sen argues that the idea of merit and its relationship with justice is vitally connected with objectives.[85] To act effectively, managers must formulate some view of what is happening. They need to assemble available evidence into a coherent picture, which indicates what action should be taken. To do so, they must know at what they are aiming. Managers need the equivalent of the physician's aim of health.

Organizational ethics would therefore put ethicists in the business of specifying and justifying substantive aims for organizations, their stakeholders, and their managers to pursue. Collins and Porras[86] argue that "visionary companies" are characterized by adherence to some core guiding set of values—and, importantly, that shareholder wealth maximization is typically not among such values. Aims are not only allowable within organizations, but they also provide a positive contribution to their success.

In business, the aim is assumed to be economic performance, or task completion in service of that end. However, if we want managers to retain "double vision"[87] (commitment to a particular view of things simultaneous with an openness to alternative possibilities) and if they are to remain sensitive to the ethical dimensions of their environment, and to act in an ethical manner, then ethicists need to supply substantive ethical aims, alongside the procedures, constraints, and "thou shall nots" we are more comfortable identifying. Specifying aims promises to keep ethical considerations alive in organizations, because it coincides with powerful currents of individual and organizational psychology.[88] As a result, the reasons that may drive us to insist that states abstain from endorsing specific ends may be the same reasons that drive us to have organizations actively promote specific aims. Among the aims organizations should pursue are those of the various stakeholders of the organization.

The existence of aims is among the important features of organizations that distinguish them from nation-states. Given this, it makes sense that organizational ethics focus to some degree on what these aims might usefully be rather than (to repeat) simply delineate "thou shall nots."[89]

Conceptual Independence   Organizational ethics must rest on its own logic and assumptions, grounded in the distinctive attributes that make them organizations. This is not to say that organizational ethics must be militantly autonomous. Organizational ethics may reasonably—indeed must—draw upon predecessor moral and political theories. However, it should neither assume an idealized political arrangement and perfect deliberative agents nor be dependent upon any one moral or political theory. Rather, a robust organizational ethics would be consistent with a plurality of moral and political views.

The principle of stakeholder fairness elaborated herein is consistent with multiple moral and political theories. It is Rawlsian in provenance and derivation and may rely upon "justice as fairness" for its politico-moral grounding. However, it is not, therefore, inconsistent with other comprehensive moral schemes. In contrast to theories that posit social contracts and community norms, fair play requires none of the assumptions implicit in these other theories (e.g., that a just ordering of society already undergirds economic interaction). Rather, whatever the background conditions, the derivation of benefits from a joint economic endeavor carries with it certain obligations, and contributing to the endeavor proffers certain rights. Stakeholder theory is independent of any single moral theory.

If one's politico-moral theory already entails such rights and obligations as *person* or as *citizen*, then the principle of stakeholder fairness merely reinforces the existence of such obligations. It provides a buttressing account of their moral weight in the economic realm of activity. It even serves as a counterweight to claims of superceding ownership rights and fiduciary duties. However, if one's politico-moral views are more minimalist (libertarian, for example[90]), then the principle of stakeholder fairness describes how the voluntary actions of organizational actors *create* the more extensive rights and obligations—*qua* organizational stakeholder—assumed on a "thicker" politico-moral theory. Hence, an appropriately independent theory of organizational ethics can appeal to a plurality of political and moral points of view without necessitating assumptions about prior political conditions and individual attributes, and without depending upon a justification lodged in a particular political or moral theory.

However, it may be objected that such a theory of organizational ethics is merely a parasitic extension of moral and political philosophy and is not as independent as the preceding would suggest. This is an interesting criticism worthy of brief discussion as it also helps bring out an important point regarding two-tiered models such as Rawls's justice as fairness, Donaldson and Dunfee's ISCT, and the principle of stakeholder fairness described herein.

The term *parasitic* carries with it a negative connotation of something nonreciprocal, unoriginal, unnecessary, and unhelpful. The parasite lives off of the host and contributes nothing to that host. Merely reading from the classics in moral and political philosophy and inserting *corporation* for *nation-state* and *stakeholder* for *citizen* without adding any additional value could possibly be construed as parasitic upon such classics. However, this is not what it is suggested a rich theory of organizational ethics should do. Rather, such a theory ought to be both responsive and instructive toward the needs of *persons in organizations* as well as complementary to the work of political philosophers. The theory elaborated here picks up the Rawlsian thread where Rawls himself leaves off. As such, rather than parasitic, the relationship is better described as symbiotic.

Organizational and politico-moral philosophy contribute to the richness of one another. Much political philosophy employs a rather impoverished view of the corporation[91] if not one that is explicitly hostile to the concentration of power that modern corporations represent. Such a picture need not be the case. Many organizations have quite a positive impact on society. In either case, a rich political theory of contemporary relevance must account for moral actions in an organizational context. Similarly, organizations necessarily exist within the space of the moral and political and must take account of these demands. This is the essence of the two-tiered approach.

The call for organizational ethics is not a call to ignore important issues at a higher level than that of individual organizations. Obviously, moral and political theory will be of use at this higher level. Indeed, stakeholder theory may provide helpful detail to a political theory that takes seriously the role of business and other organizations in political society. Rawlsian devices or those of other politico-moral theories would be useful, for example, in establishing the law of corporations. These uses would not run contrary to the previous arguments, because the discussion concerns the set of all corporations rather than the obligations of any single organization. This use is consistent with Rawls's limitation of his arguments to the basic structure inasmuch as the law of corporations is part of the basic structure of society.

While theorists working on questions at the organizational level of abstraction may draw on the broader notions of moral and political philosophy, this does not imply the need for a direct transposition of concepts and method from one level of abstraction to another. In his 1974 presidential address to the American Philosophical Association, entitled "The Independence of Moral Theory," Rawls argues against the idea that there is a hierarchy within philosophy in which "[m]oral philosophy is then viewed as secondary to metaphysics and the philosophy of mind as well, which are in turn secondary to the theory of meaning and epistemology."[92] Analogous to the relationship between classical politico-moral theory and organizational ethics proposed here, he goes on to write:

> . . . moral theory is, in important respects, independent from certain philosophical subjects sometimes regarded as methodologi-

cally prior to it. But I do not care for independence too strictly understood; an idea I like better is that each part of philosophy should have its own subject and problems and yet, at the same time, stand directly or indirectly in relations of mutual dependence with the others. The fault of methodological hierarchies is not unlike the fault of political and social ones: they lead to a distortion of vision with a consequent misdirection of effort.[93]

Conclusion

Markets have already attracted great attention from philosophers and economists,[94] and though organizational ethics might offer a distinctive perspective on market activity, I have focused on the other, all-but-ignored engines of economic activity, organizations. What is needed, however, is not that ethicists simply consider organizations; rather, that organizations require an ethics of their own, an ethics that reflects the significant differences that distinguish them from the nation-state and individuals.

The remainder of the current project represents arguments in favor of a theory of organizational ethics of the sort called for in this chapter. I will argue that *stakeholder theory*—founded upon a principle of stakeholder fairness—provides a useful moral framework at the organizational level. The next chapter will examine the history of stakeholder theory and suggest a number of shortcomings that must be addressed for the theory to advance.

CHAPTER 4

Stakeholder Theory and Its Critics

E thics has long been a part of the study of economics and commercial interaction. Adam Smith and John Stuart Mill (to name but two of the better known) are as well known for their thinking on matters of moral philosophy as they are of their work on political economy. As the study of economics proceeded, however, it became an ever more technical discipline with the concomitant deemphasis of that which could not be measured, including concern over morals. In *On Ethics and Economics*, Nobel laureate Amartya Sen comments unfavorably on the schism that has evolved between the two intimately connected disciplines. Sen writes:

> [T]he subject of ethics was for a long time seen as something like a branch of economics. . . . In fact, in the 1930's when Lionel Robbins in his influential book *An Essay on the Nature and Significance of Economic Science*, argued that "it does not seem logically possible to associate the two studies [economics and ethics] in any form but mere juxtaposition,"[95] he was taking a position that was quite unfashionable then, though extremely fashionable now.[96]

This technical preoccupation continued in much of what would become management and organization studies. Though concerned in some measure with creating a "just system" of deriving a "fair" wage,[97] Frederick Winslow Taylor's scientific management was predominantly a technical undertaking. Henry Towne's "The Engineer as Economist" has emerged as a classic piece in the organization studies literature.[98] Notwithstanding the work of pioneers such as Mary Parker Follett[99] and Chester Barnard[100] on the human dimensions of management, the technical aspects continued to play a prominent role in management and organization studies throughout the latter half of the twentieth century.

This preoccupation with quantitative approaches to management continued even as attention to the social responsibilities of business began to reemerge. Extensive work has been undertaken which attempts to determine what, if any, relationship exists between organizational ethics and other quantitative measures of corporate success. Margolis and Walsh[101] recently completed a comprehensive review of the literature (thirty years and ninety-five empirical studies) on the relationship between corporate social responsibility and profitability. They conclude that "the existing body of work cannot be relied upon for answers."[102] Further, there should be a reorientation of the research program relating to corporate social performance and corporate social responsibility. They ask and answer, "Would evidence of an empirical link, one way or the other, fundamentally change these [socially responsible] investment decisions? We think not" (p. 25). The following passage from Tetlock[103] is instructive:

> [D]isagreements rooted in values should be profoundly resistant to change. . . . Libertarian conservatives might oppose the (confiscatory) stakeholder model even when confronted by evidence that concessions in this direction have no adverse effect on profitability to shareholders. Expropriation is expropriation, no matter how prettified. And some egalitarians might well

endorse the stakeholder model, even if shown compelling evidence that it reduces profits. Academics who rely on evidence-based appeals to change minds when the disagreements are rooted in values may be wasting everyone's time.[104]

Disagreements founded on values must be adjudicated on this same basis.

Explicit and predominant focus on the moral aspects of organizational relationships with stakeholders has never played a more prominent role than that played in contemporary stakeholder theory.[105] Not only have the past fifteen to twenty years witnessed a marked growth in the literature on stakeholder theory, but, more tellingly, there has been an increase in the *rate* of growth of stakeholder scholarship in recent years. It is fair to say that the proliferation of research undertaken under the aegis of stakeholder theory has undergone an explosion. Since the last count of "about a dozen books and more than 100 articles with primary emphasis on the stakeholder concept,"[106] a comprehensive bibliography has become nearly impossible. The stakeholder idea has also spread from the realm of scholarly literature to the arena of popular discussion. Stakeholdership is a central theme in the political discourse of the United Kingdom.[107]

Rowley's[108] social network treatment of stakeholder theory, elaborated upon by Frooman,[109] adds depth and richness to our understanding of relationships between and among stakeholders. Other work has been devoted to examining the relationship between stakeholder management and financial success.[110]

Orts thoroughly discusses treatment of stakeholders ("corporate constituencies") in the law.[111] Tracing the theoretical roots of constituency statutes to stakeholder management theory in American business schools, he observes that twenty-nine states have, as of his writing, statutes that "purport to expand the traditional view that directors of corporations have a duty to make business decisions primarily, if not exclusively, to maximize shareholders' wealth by explicitly permitting consideration of non-shareholder interests."[112] The law review literature concerning issues relating to stakeholder management is large and growing.[113] The role—or non-role—played by the law in the stakeholder theory described herein is discussed later in this chapter.

This chapter will seek to review and critically assess a small part of the literature on stakeholder theory to date. With full recognition of and appreciation for the fact that many others have discussed relationships between organizations and external constituencies before and that there is a long history of scholarship on ethics in economic contexts, the focus of this chapter will be on that stream of research that is explicitly concerned with stakeholder theory. More specifically, I am concerned with that stream of literature that takes Freeman's 1984 work as the *locus classicus*.

Freeman's study of the early history of the stakeholder concept remains unsurpassed in its comprehensiveness and depth. I would refer the reader to Freeman's study of this early history. The publication of Freeman's *Strategic Management: A Stakeholder Approach* (1984, hereafter *SMSA*) marks a consolidation of myriad works. He took the ideas of the Stanford Research Institute and the subsequent work in other areas and operationalized them into a coherent set of ideas for the practicing manager. Freeman's definition, based on "Thompson's[114] claim [that] 'stakeholder' should denote 'those groups which can make a difference,'" states:

> A stakeholder in an organization is (by definition) any group or individual who can affect or is affected by the achievement of the organization's objectives.[115]

SMSA marked the first explicit attempt to describe the stakeholder idea as an explicitly managerial approach to organizational strategy. "Stakeholder" went from being more than an intuitively appealing description of a firm's theoretically underrepresented constituencies to "stakeholder management"—a well-elaborated method of decision making in organizations. *SMSA* took the stakeholder idea to a higher level of theoretical sophistication.

Stakeholder Distinctions

The most prominent and oft-cited works in stakeholder theory suggest distinctions within the theory designed to make it more useful. In this section, I will discuss the most widely cited of these and assess the authors' claims.

Mitchell, Agle, and Wood propose a theory of stakeholder salience defined as "the degree to which priority is given to competing stakeholder claims."[116] Stakeholders and their claims are classified based on the relative presence of three characteristics: legitimacy, power, and urgency. Using these three attributes, the authors suggest a theory of stakeholder identification that is "comprehensive and useful" and attempts to bridge the "broad vs. narrow" debate. The theory of stakeholder identification and salience, and in particular the Mitchell et al. notion of stakeholder legitimacy, receives more attention in Chapter 6.

Donaldson and Preston[117] attempt to bring greater clarity and rigor to stakeholder theory by arguing for a taxonomy consisting of descriptive, instrumental, and normative varieties of research. Descriptive stakeholder research analyzes stakeholder management as it is found (or not) in actual organizations. This variety of scholarship (purportedly) makes no prescriptive or normative assertions about the desirability of stakeholder management. Instrumental stakeholder theory assesses the extent to which managing stakeholders and stakeholder relationships conduce to the achievement of commonly asserted organizational goals (e.g., profitability, maximization of shareholder or firm value, viability). Instrumental stakeholder research makes prescriptions, but does not question the moral legitimacy of the goals themselves. The purpose of the corporation is taken as self-evident. Normative stakeholder theory addresses directly the moral justification of the organization and the ethics of stakeholder management. Donaldson and Preston conclude that all three are vital to the stakeholder research program, but that the normative variety is foundational to all. They conclude by proposing a theory of property rights as one candidate normative basis for stakeholder theory.

Jones and Wicks[118] argue for a convergent stakeholder theory. They provide an outstanding description of the variety of questions to which stakeholder theory aspires to respond and the disparate standards of evaluation that apply to these questions and their answers. They also propose a plausible amalgamated solution to the perceived disparity between the normative and instrumental streams of research. In a sense, they can be seen as resynthesizing that which Donaldson and Preston analyzed.

In his response to Jones and Wicks, and indirectly in response to Donaldson and Preston, Freeman[119] casts doubt upon the descriptive/instrumental/normative taxonomy itself and hence the usefulness of convergent stakeholder theory. He writes:

> [I]f we drop the tripartite typology of Donaldson & Preston, then plainly there is no need for anything like convergent stakeholder theory. There is nothing to converge—no separate contributions for philosophers and management theorists. There are just narratives about stakeholders and narratives about these narratives—that is, theory. The overwhelming logic to drop this distinction is pretty simple. By choosing to call groups "stakeholders," rather than "interest groups," "constituencies," or "publics," we have already mixed up "fact" and "value." *Stakeholder* is an obvious literary device meant to call into question the emphasis on "stockholders." The very idea of a purely descriptive, value-free, or value-neutral stakeholder theory is a contradiction in terms.[120]

Implicit in Jones and Wicks's convergent solution, then, is the idea that the two research streams—normative ethics and social science—were never as far apart as some scholars would have us believe. Freeman, therefore, has a point. It is unfortunate that such an article as "Convergent Stakeholder Theory" had to be written at all. Moral theory with no reference to our world is empty formalism; value-free science is impossible. These are not, however, universally held ideas; stakeholder theory has provided fodder and a battleground for those who believe in the strict partitioning of knowledge.

Part of the contribution of distinctions like those of Donaldson and Preston and Mitchell, Agle, and Wood is that they facilitate a division of labor among those with myriad scholarly strengths (e.g., quantitative, logical, narrative). An unfortunate side effect of such typologies is that, rather than using them to create an area of common ground among people using different methods, it frequently allows these people to slip back into their cozy and familiar ways of thinking and to continue to speak past one another with merely a new vocabulary. Old wine in new wineskins.

This having been said, these distinctions and typologies have made a contribution. The conversation that motivated "Convergent Stakeholder Theory" had to occur. The divisions were (perhaps continue to be) too deep for stakeholder theory to immediately take root the way Freeman envisioned (and continues to envision). The *separation* was inevitable due to the prevailing background conditions and training of the parties involved. Creating a language to talk about this separation has prompted a more thorough elaboration and defense of Freeman's monolith. In at least this way, the analyses of Donaldson and Preston and Mitchell, Agle, and Wood, as well as the synthesis of Jones and Wicks, have done a service to the theory and the field.[121] The discussion of stakeholder legitimacy in Chapter 6 aspires to demonstrate how a distinction can add clarity to a topic—even if that clarity is achieved through a taxonomic critique. As Freeman indicates, the integration was there all along, but history was such that the full significance of this integration required time and thought to proliferate.

Stakeholders, Agency Theory, and Fiduciary Duties

Another approach to the study of stakeholder theory is comparing it to more traditional theories of economics. Agency defenses and critiques of stakeholder theory have been among the most widely discussed in the literature.[122,123] As a corollary to the principle-agent controversy in stakeholder theory, much controversy exists concerning the role of fiduciary duties within stakeholder theory.[124] According to various authors, either

1. Fiduciary duties extend to all stakeholders in a "multi-fiduciary" fashion,[125]
2. Multi-fiduciary duties are impossible,[126] thus creating a "stakeholder paradox,"[127]
3. Fiduciary duties are a public policy expedient,[128] or
4. Fiduciary duties are irrelevant to the topic of stakeholder theory and practice.[129]

These conclusions and the arguments leading up to them mark one of the central disputes in stakeholder theory.

Goodpaster posits a "stakeholder paradox":

> It seems essential, yet in some ways illegitimate, to orient corporate decisions by ethical values that go beyond strategic stakeholder considerations to multi-fiduciary ones.[130]

Strategic stakeholder considerations are those that concern stakeholders only to the extent that they may have an impact on the firm's traditionally measured economic performance. Multi-fiduciary considerations, on the other hand, dictate that stakeholders merit consideration in their own right.

Goodpaster's article in which the stakeholder paradox is elaborated—bolstered by Marcoux, Maitland, and a response article of his own—sparked an interesting and ongoing debate among theorists regarding the fiduciary status of share owners and stakeholders. Responding to Goodpaster, Boatright argues that there is nothing remarkable about share owners that makes them the preeminent stakeholder group and thus denies the existence of the paradox.[131] He examines the claim that the relationship between a corporation's officers and directors and its share owners is "ethically different" from the relationship between managers and other constituencies. Morally significant differences between the two types of relationships would tend to bolster the fiduciary argument against stakeholder theory, while the absence of such moral differences would severely damage this argument. Though I use Boatright's article as a framework for examining the question of fiduciary duties and stakeholder theory, not all of the arguments presented are his.

In asking, "What's so special about stakeholders?" Boatright examines three possibilities for rendering morally different the relationship between managers and share owners from those of other constituencies: property, contractual relations, and agency. In his discussion of property rights, Boatright looks closely at what he calls "the equity argument," an argument he attributes to Oliver Williamson. The argument is that a share owner's investment is different from that which is invested by other constituencies in that "[t]he whole of their investment in the firm is potentially placed at hazard." That is, "[t]hey are the only voluntary constituency whose relation with the corporation does not come up for periodic renewal." Therefore, on Williamson's account, share owners need additional protection of some kind.

In response, Boatright questions the need for the protection of fiduciary duties in addition to existing share owner rights. In other words, share owners already have rights that will protect them from the larger part of the hazards created by Williamson's "equity argument." Examples of such existing rights are the right to elect boards of directors and vote on share owner resolutions. In light of these rights, Boatright finds unnecessary—or at least in need of further justification—the "more stringent fiduciary duty."[132]

One possible criticism of Boatright on this argument regards the basis for these existing share owner rights. To what extent are these rights themselves derived from some property or fiduciary right? The rights to vote for boards of directors and share owner resolutions do not sound like rights that would qualify as foundational moral rights. Rather, they would seem to be derived from some other more basic right. If they are unjustified standing alone, then does Boatright actually have an argument against the need to protect share owners' rights? Unless Boatright is able to found these rights on something other than the property rights or fiduciary duties against which he is arguing, this particular part of his discussion may do little damage to either Williamson's or Goodpaster's arguments. However, Boatright has a second, more convincing, response.

Making similar arguments to those of Freeman and Evan, and Blair,[133] Boatright's second response to Williamson's "equity argument" is that the existence of a market for shares provides a great deal of security. The share owner is able to, at minimal cost, dispose of a disappointing stock and, hence, perpetually and constantly renegotiate her relationship with the corporation. Additionally, the market makes portfolio diversification possible, thus reducing further the risk to the share owner.

Marcoux responds to this "ready-market-for-shares" argument by suggesting that exclusive reliance on it reduces the applicability of stakeholder theory to only large, publicly traded corporations and that stakeholder theorists must accede fiduciary duties to shareholders in all other instances. He writes: "Sole proprietorships, partnerships, many (though not all) limited partnerships, and closely-held corporations all typically lack a developed and ready market for their equity."[134] The ready-market-for-shares argument is resistant to this response for several reasons. Most obviously, Marcoux's examples of sole proprietorships and partnerships are not subject to agency problems or fiduciary duties to the same extent as the widely or publicly held corporation, even on his own vulnerability-based account. The degree of separation of risk bearing and decision making is far less or nonexistent; nor is the level of vulnerability as high because the residual risk bearers and managers are coextensive.

The second possible justification for fiduciary duties to share owners discussed by Boatright is that of a contract. At the outset, Boatright establishes that there is no *express* contract. Rather, the contract is taken as *implied* as recognized in U.S. law. However, Boatright finds the case for an implied legal contract as "not very promising." His reasons include the lack of an agreement beyond the prospectus, the attitude of share owners as "investors" rather than "owners," and "lack of any specific representations by management to individual shareholders."[135] The contract may, however, be an implied contract of a nonlegal variety and may in this way justify the fiduciary duties to shareholders. Chapter 5 herein contains a more thorough discussion of implied contracts and tacit consent. It is argued that implied consent provides little or no justification—for either stakeholder theory or fiduciary duties. Thus, the implied contract justification of fiduciary duties is found wanting by both Boatright and myself.

The third of Boatright's candidates for justifying a moral distinction between share owners and stakeholders is agency. Justification for fiduciary duties is commonly thought to arise due to the agency relationship between share owners and managers.[a] Fiduciary duties may, therefore, arise due to the agency relationship between managers and shareholders; however, no such agency relationship exists. Boatright follows Clark, who writes:

---

[a]Or sometimes vice versa with fiduciary duties creating agency relationships.

To an experienced corporate lawyer who has studied primary legal materials, the assertion that corporate managers are agents of investors, whether debtholders or stockholders, will seem odd or loose. The lawyer would make the following points: (1) corporate officers like the president and treasurer are agents of the corporation itself; (2) the board of directors is the ultimate decision-making body of the corporation (and in a sense is the group most appropriately identified with "the corporation"); (3) directors are not agents of the corporation but are sui generis; (4) neither officers nor directors are agents of the stockholders; but (5) both officers and directors are "fiduciaries" with respect to the corporation and its stockholders.[136]

According to the definition of agency found in the second *Restatement of Agency*, Section 1(1), the defining characteristics are: "(1) consent to the relation, (2) the power to act on another's behalf, and (3) element of control." Though these characteristics may exist between top management/directors and the corporation, they do not exist between managers and shareholders. It then becomes a matter of how one delimits the corporation.[137]

In an ingenious article, Thomas A. Smith argues for a "neo-traditional interpretation of fiduciary duty."[138] He uses a hypothetical bargaining situation to determine what sort of fiduciary duties would be selected *ex ante* as contractual "gap-filling principles" to the "standard form contract" of corporate law. He contends that the shareholder wealth maximization imperative is actually inefficient and would not be chosen by rational bargaining parties. Rather, parties bargaining rationally—in this case rationality is determined by consistency with the capital asset pricing model (CAPM)—would have fiduciary duties extend to the firm itself rather than to shareholders alone. Maximization of firm value, defined as the totality of all financial claims against the firm, would supplant shareholder wealth maximization as the objective function of the firm. Smith calls this norm according to which fiduciary duties run to the corporation rather than the shareholders neotraditional because of the following:

> Until well into this century, lawyers and judges conceived of the corporate fiduciary duty as running to "the corporation" itself rather than primarily or exclusively to the shareholders.[139]

Smith's arguments bear brief recapitulation here.

There is an established exception in corporate law to the shareholder wealth maximization norm. When a corporation is close to insolvency (i.e., "vicinity of insolvency"), managers have an incentive to undertake unusually risky projects to maintain the corporation as a viable, going concern.

> In the Credit Lyonnais case, Chancellor William Allen opined that "in the vicinity of insolvency," the fiduciary duty "shifts" from being owed to shareholders to being owed to creditors.[140,141]

When faced with insolvency or taking on final, high-risk effort to save the company, managers have incentives toward the latter. This can be harmful to holders of other financial instruments, such as bonds, if this last-gasp effort fails. The shareholders are little worse off because their investment was in grave danger whether the risky project is undertaken or not. A failure of the risky project may significantly reduce the amount left for other bond holders, however. Maximizing shareholder wealth would dictate undertaking the project without extra-contractual (fiduciary) duty to bond holders. Hence, limiting managerial discretion in the "vicinity of insolvency" improves overall efficiency.

Smith suggests, however, that "firms are always in the vicinity of insolvency because all it takes for any firm, no matter how solvent, to become insolvent is to lose a sufficiently risky bet."[142] A manager motivated by maximizing shareholder wealth, primarily or exclusively, will have incentives to undertake such particularly risky projects.

For example, take a very solvent firm ABC, which has assets of $100 million and liabilities of $10 million. By making a highly leveraged bet in, say, the derivative market, it would have, let us suppose, a one in one hundred chance of gaining $10 billion, and a 99 percent chance of losing the firm's entire value. This bet would have a present value of $10.9 million to shareholders while it would have an expected value to the corporation of only $1 million. The price of this lottery-ticket-like bet is, let us suppose, $10 million. Thus is has a net expected value to the corporation of negative $9 million—obviously a bad bet for the firm.[143]

This is not, however, a bad bet for the shareholders. The implication of this argument is that the vicinity of insolvency is ubiquitous. As such, the "vicinity of insolvency" exception in which fiduciary duties extend to other claimants on the corporation, may be widely or universally applicable.

Smith goes on to argue that economically and financially rational parties, according to the CAPM, will own a "market portfolio" of not only equity shares, but all varieties of financial instruments available. If these rational individuals, each holding the market portfolio of investments, were to negotiate *ex ante* for gap-filling principles, then one such principle would not be maximizing shareholder wealth. The rational investor would own not only stocks, but also bonds and other forms of debt. They would not want to see the equity investment (i.e., common stock) privileged to the detriment of these other forms of debt unless the increase in the value of the equity were greater than the decrease in the value of the other forms of debt. In other words, rational investors would demand managerial decisions that enhance the net value of the gamut of corporate obligations. Rational investors would want managers to act so as to maximize the value of all claims on the corporation. Thus, like the traditional norm, the neotraditional fiduciary norm that such negotiators would settle upon would be a duty to the corporation rather than equity shareholders.

The final prong of Smith's argument is that the increasing complexity of financial markets and instruments (e.g., derivatives, tracking stock, "letter stocks" of different classes) make it concomitantly more difficult to determine who is the equity shareholder and thus to whom a fiduciary duty is due under a system of shareholder wealth maximization. The practical difficulties with ascertaining the identity of this group will only become greater as financing arrangements become more and more complex. Duties running to shareholders alone are therefore theoretically inferior and less practicable in adjudication.

Notably for the purposes of this book, Smith places limitations on his theory writing, "This does not mean, however, that with no additional theoretical warrant, we can somehow extend the analysis to all providers of input to the firm."[144] In other words, the neotraditional norm Smith sketches does not automatically extend to nonfinancial stakeholders. (Nor do I make such a claim on Smith's behalf.) The reasons for elaborating upon his ideas are:

1. To demonstrate the viability of duties running to the corporation. Such duties are not an anachronism of the early twentieth century and before, but the subject of serious and compelling recent scholarship.
2. To contribute further to the dispatching of the mistaken notion of a moral duty running primarily or exclusively to equity shareholders, thus creating space for obligations of stakeholder fairness.

Only under the assumption that *the corporation is the same thing as its shareholders* are arguments for agency-based fiduciary duties to shareholders viable. Directors and top management indeed have fiduciary duties to the organization on behalf of which they act; but this does not imply a fiduciary duty or agency relationship between managers and shareholders—or between management and any other stakeholder. Even the (wrong) assumption that shareholders *own* the corporation does not imply coextension. Shareholders own nothing more than the right to a residual cash flow and even in this they enjoy limited liability. "[D]irectors and top managers can neither bind individual shareholders to contracts with third parties or [sic] generate personal liabilities for them through debt or tort. On the other hand, directors (and *their* agents, high level managers) *can* legally bind the corporate entity as a whole to either contractual obligations or financial liability."[145] Managers are not agents of share owners, share owners do not own the corporation, and less still are share owners coextensive with the corporation. The agency defense of fiduciary duties to share owners fails. Indeed, Marens and Wicks conclude that fiduciary duties are irrelevant to managerial decision making and present no obstacle to stakeholder management—the "stakeholder paradox" does not exist.

None of this necessarily condemns "agency" explanations and analyses in the economics literature as long as one is careful in moving between economic, legal, and moral conceptions. The analysis of "agency costs" is a powerful explanatory tool of economic analysis. The agency theorists' explanations of residual claims and monitoring costs are all powerful and insightful. None of this necessarily leads to the conclusion that shareholders own the corporation in any meaningful sense, nor that managers are agents of shareholder principals with concomitant fiduciary duties. The problem arises when the moral implications of "agency" are assumed based on this economic analysis rather than carefully considered. Legitimate agency relationships (e.g., in the legal sense adumbrated in Clark's previous statement) and fiduciary duties imply legal and moral obligations.[146] It is this conceptual leap from residual claimant to owner, facilitated by calling the model "agency" theory and stipulating shareholders as "owners," that is unjustified.

Marcoux is among the stakeholder critics careful to elaborate and defend the idea of fiduciary duties to shareholders from a moral perspective. His article, entitled "A Fiduciary Argument Against Stakeholder Theory," is the most recent installment in the "stakeholder paradox" dispute and bears a brief examination in light of the preceding discussion. An analysis of his arguments should help us to determine the nature of the relationship between stakeholder theory and fiduciary duties. (Recall the possibilities from the beginning of this section: Fiduciary duties extend to all stakeholders, apply only to shareholders, are merely a public policy expedient with no moral depth, or are generally irrelevant to stakeholder theory.)

In his article, Marcoux is primarily concerned with dispelling the idea of multi-fiduciary stakeholder theory (i.e., the idea that managers bear fiduciary duties to all stakeholders and not to shareholders alone) apparently as part of a larger project of dismantling stakeholder theory entirely. He begins by demonstrating the conceptual and practical impossibility of multiple fiduciary duties among potentially competing parties. For the purposes of a particular project, the fiduciary must put the interests of the beneficiary ahead of all others including her own. But it is impossible to put the competing interest of any one beneficiary ahead of all others while putting each of the others ahead of this same beneficiary as well as all others. "In other words, the nature of the fiduciary relation is such that it is impossible for one to act as a fiduciary for multiple parties where the interests of those parties are (or are likely to be) in conflict."[147] He concludes, therefore, that the obligations of stakeholder theory are necessarily non-fiduciary in nature.

Fiduciary duties are nevertheless morally deep, Marcoux continues. The arguments of "moral depth" of fiduciary duties are in response to Boatright's contention that the best way to understand fiduciary duties in the context of stakeholder theory is as a public policy issue. Boatright adopts a middle ground in the stakeholder paradox debate by concluding that there is nothing special about shareholders that entitle them to differential treatment by managers, but that fiduciary duties are nevertheless important from a public policy perspective. He writes:

> On questions about the nature and structure of the corporation, with which fiduciary duties are largely concerned, courts and legislatures have held, for reasons of public policy, that the profit-making function of corporations and accountability to shareholders ought to be preserved. On the questions of ordinary business operation, however, public policy dictates that corporations be allowed to take the interests of many constituencies beside the shareholders into account.[148]

Marcoux objects to this conclusion by taking seriously the moral aspects of agency theory and fiduciary duties. He argues that the "special vulnerability" of one party to another creates a fiduciary relationship between them. It is wrong for more than legal and public policy reasons for a doctor to act in her own interest at the expense of patient health. There is a morally deep fiduciary relationship that exists between doctor and patient. Marcoux's argument is sound up to this point.

Central to Marcoux's argument is that such duties exist not only in the doctor–patient, attorney–client, and guardian–ward relationships, but also in the manager–shareholder relationship. It is not sufficient to merely point out that some fiduciary duties are morally deep and that stakeholder theory is nonfiduciary. The stakeholder theorist may concede these points, and still argue—for the same reasons cited by Boatright, and Marens and Wicks—that there is no special fiduciary duty between shareholders and managers. The general irrelevance argument may still hold.

Marcoux must therefore claim that not only is there something morally deep about fiduciary duties, but also that such duties exist between managers and *shareholders*. Here his argument falls victim to the error of coextension as previously described. Managers do indeed bear a fiduciary duty, but it is to the corporation, not to the shareholders; the two are not the same. Fiduciary duties are not entirely irrelevant. For all of the reasons cited by stakeholder critics (e.g., accountability, avoiding managerial opportunism, and self-dealing), fiduciary duties have a role to play in stakeholder theory. The key is in accurately determining the beneficiary. The duty is owed by managers and directors to the organization rather than to the shareholders or any other single stakeholder group. Consider in defense of this claim that a derivative lawsuit is typically brought by a shareholder against an opportunistic manager or director *on behalf of the corporation.* The standing of the plaintiff is derivative, not direct.[b]

This conflation of shareholders with corporation appears throughout Marcoux's article. For example, in indicating the "special vulnerability" of shareholders to managers, he writes:

> Shareholders suffer the special disadvantage of having *their* assets in the hands of a management team in possession of all of the relevant knowledge, in control of all aspects of *their* investment, and in control of the flow of information to the shareholders.[149]

If care were taken to distinguish shareholder from corporation, we would see that the shareholders, in fact, continue to control the *stock* that is both their asset and their investment. The assets Marcoux describes as being under the control of management are the assets of the organization, not the shareholders.

Stakeholder Theory and the Place of Fairness

From the introductory chapter and the preceding review of the stakeholder literature, the reader should have a good idea about the aspects of stakeholder theory that are being

---

[b]It would be interesting, though outside the scope of this chapter, to consider the implications of granting legal standing to stakeholders in derivative lawsuits as a way of ensuring accountability. If this legal right were extended (possibly one at a time beginning with employees) to other stakeholders, managerial accountability would be maintained, as would the agency relationship between managers (agents) and the corporation (principal) within a stakeholder legal regime.

addressed in this book. However, for the sake of clarity, this section will discuss the shortcomings in stakeholder theory that were the impetus for this and much of the work discussed herein. Among these problems are the lack of a normative, justificatory framework and the problem of stakeholder identity. I shall briefly lay out the problems here.

Thomas Donaldson has written:

> Despite its important insights, the stakeholder model has serious problems. The two most obvious are its inability to provide standards for assigning relative weights to the interests of the various constituencies, and its failure to contain within itself, or make reference to, a normative, justificatory foundation.[150]

This criticism and others like it were the motivation for the current project. That is, even if the "Foundation" of stakeholder theory eludes us, there may, nonetheless, be a deeper normative justification for stakeholder obligations than currently exists in the literature. The arguments that follow are intended to provide such a deeper justification.

Freeman defines a stakeholder as "any group or individual who can affect or is affected by the achievement of the firm's objectives."[151] He effectively demonstrates why persons or groups of the former type (i.e., those who can affect the firm) demand attention. The arguments are straightforwardly prudential in nature and seem to view stakeholders instrumentally. This much seems clear; to the extent that there are persons or groups who can affect the accomplishment of one's goals, one would be prudentially remiss if she failed to include the possible effects of these groups in her calculations. More troublesome for Freeman's prudential treatment is accounting for those who are affected by, but do not significantly affect, a firm's operations. Freeman explains:

> [I]t is less obvious why "those groups who are affected by the corporation" are stakeholders as well, for not all groups who can affect the corporation are themselves affected by the firm. I

make the definition symmetric because of the changes which the firm has undergone in the past few years. Groups which 20 years ago had no effect on the actions of the firm, can affect it today, largely because of the actions of the firm which ignored the actions of these groups. Thus, by calling those affected groups "stakeholders," the ensuing strategic management model will be sensitive to future change . . .[152]

Freeman thus tries to reduce all stakeholder interest into prudential interest by claiming that those whom the corporation affects may some day come to affect the firm's operations. Insofar as this "prudential stakeholder model" relies only on considerations of organizational well-being,[153] it may be perfectly consistent with the claim that a manager's only obligation is to increase profits. Such a model is insufficient as a basis of normative organizational ethics study. This book suggests that a principle of fairness provides a normative basis for stakeholder claims aside from prudential interests.

Secondly, stakeholder theory as currently discussed has no means of determining who are and who are not stakeholders in the moral sense. This is the problem of stakeholder identity. It has been suggested that groups as disparate as activists, competitors,[154] and the natural environment[155] be considered stakeholders. In fact, it would seem that current theory is unable to rule out *any* group from stakeholder status. If the fact that a group may some day come to affect the achievement of an organization's objectives qualifies that group as a stakeholder, who or what fails to qualify? Inability to properly discern stakeholders from non-stakeholders threatens the meaningfulness of the term. If everyone is a stakeholder of everyone else, what value is added through use of the term *stakeholder*? The principle of stakeholder fairness more clearly defines the concept of stakeholder in such a way as to distinguish which groups are and which are not stakeholders in the sense of having additional moral obligations over and above those one is presumed to have to human beings in general.

This brings up a final important point that should be made explicit and will be repeated throughout. Stakeholder status as here conceived indicates the presence of an *additional* obligation over and above that due others simply by virtue of being human. When it is indicated that a particular group is not a stakeholder group, it would be a mistake to take this to mean that the organization has *no* moral relationship with that group. Simply because a person or group does not merit the additional moral consideration conferred by stakeholder status does not mean that they may be morally disregarded. One still may not break promises without sufficient cause, torture for fun, or otherwise act immorally toward non-stakeholders. However, no *additional* moral consideration is due non-stakeholders group in managerial decision making. It is a group's engagement in and acceptance of the benefits of a cooperative scheme that creates the extra obligation owed to such groups by managers. Considering a group a stakeholder, on this conception, is to consider that group as meriting *extra* consideration due to the presence of an additional obligation. To deny that a group merits stakeholder status is not to take anything away from that group, but rather to deny the existence of such an additional obligation.

Conclusion

This chapter has examined a portion of the extant stakeholder literature. A critical assessment of some particularly relevant literature to current purposes reveals a number of conceptual shortcomings. Donaldson has suggested that the failure of stakeholder theory to make reference to a normative grounding is among the greatest problems for stakeholder theory; and Donaldson and Preston argue that the normative category of stakeholder literature is the most basic of the three categories in their taxonomy. The absence of a rigorous normative underpinning represents not only a gap in the theory in itself, but also leads to other theoretical ambiguities such as the problem of stakeholder identification.

I have attempted to show how these conceptual gaps can be problematic for stakeholder theory as well as how a principle of stakeholder fairness may serve to fill these gaps in a way that compares favorably with extant stakeholder writings. However, this comparison to other theories may seem premature inasmuch as the reader has to this point been provided with only a skeletal elaboration and justification of the principle itself from the introductory chapter. The next chapter will attempt to provide a more thorough discussion of and arguments for the principle of stakeholder fairness. I implore the skeptical reader to reconsider the comparisons made in this chapter with other stakeholder writings after having explored the principle in greater detail.

CHAPTER 5

A Principle of Stakeholder Fairness

To this point I have argued that the ethical issues that arise at the organizational level of abstraction are sufficiently different from the problems addressed by standard moral and political philosophy to justify an explicitly organizational-level moral theory.[156] I have further suggested—but have yet to argue—that stakeholder theory provides a strong candidate for just such an organizational-level moral theory. In the preceding chapter I pointed out some conceptual shortcomings in need of remedy if stakeholder theory is to adequately serve as a framework for organizational ethics.

In the present chapter I turn to an explication and defense of a principle that fills the conceptual gaps noted in the previous chapter. I argue for a principle of stakeholder fairness based on Rawls's principle of fair play as a moral foundation of stakeholder theory.

A Principle of Fairness

While H.L.A. Hart is most often credited with the first explicit, contemporary discussion of the idea in 1955,[157] obligations and duties similar to those based on fair play were discussed by John Stuart Mill in 1859.

> When a person, either by express promise or by conduct, has encouraged another to rely upon his continuing to act in a certain way—to build expectations and calculations, and stake any part of his plan of life upon that supposition—a new series of moral obligations arises on his part towards that person, which may possibly be overruled, but cannot be ignored. ... A person is bound to take all these circumstances into account, before resolving on a step which may affect such important interests of theirs; and if he does not allow proper weight to those interests, he is morally responsible for the wrong.[158]

The principle of fair play finds further elaboration in the works of John Rawls, A. John Simmons, Kent Greenawalt, George Klosko, and Nien-hê Hsieh among many others.[159] Rawls describes the principle as follows:

> Suppose there is a mutually beneficial and just scheme of cooperation, and that the advantages it yields can only be obtained if everyone, or nearly everyone, cooperates. Suppose further that cooperation requires a certain sacrifice from each person, or at least involves a certain restriction of his liberty. Suppose finally that the benefits produced by cooperation are, up to a certain point, free: that is, the scheme of cooperation is unstable in the sense that if any one person knows that all (or nearly all) of the others will continue to do their part, he will still be able to share a gain from the scheme even if he does not do his part. Under these conditions a person who has accepted the benefits of the scheme is bound by a duty of fair play to do his part and not to take advantage of the free benefit by not cooperating.[160]

Taking this definition as a good starting point, I would now like to analyze obligations of fairness.[161] From Rawls's description we can isolate six qualifications for consideration as a cooperative scheme in which the duty of fair play is operative:

   a. Mutual benefit
   b. Justice
   c. Benefits that accrue only under conditions of near una-
      nimity of cooperation
   d. Cooperation that requires sacrifice or restriction of lib-
      erty on the part of participants
   e. The possibility of free-riders
   f. Voluntary acceptance of benefits of cooperative scheme

My aim in analyzing this definition is threefold: (1) to clarify the implications of the principle of fairness, (2) to show how it may be constructively altered, and (3) to determine the extent to which commercial exchanges may be considered the proper subject of such obligations of fairness.

    a. **Mutual benefit**   The idea of commerce as being to the mutual benefit of the participants is as old as economics. Indeed, it is the foundation of the oft-quoted passage in Smith's *Wealth of Nations* concerning the butcher, brewer, and baker.[162] In addition, "benefit" need not be a direct personal benefit to the cooperator. Benefit may include other directed desires in addition to purely egoistic ones. For instance, if a person is engaged in a cooperative scheme to obtain a benefit for her child or friend, then the scheme may still be considered mutually beneficial for current purposes.

    b. **Justice**   The second requisite feature of an appropriate cooperative scheme is that it be relatively just. As my focus is on the organizational cooperative scheme and there are many who seriously question the justness of free market economies (or at least the capitalist version of it practiced in the United States and much of the world), this condition could have a serious impact on arguments herein. Rawls defends the justness condition by claiming:

> It is generally agreed that extorted promises are void *ab initio*. But similarly, unjust social arrangements are themselves a kind of extortion, even violence, and consent to them does not bind.[163]

The problem with this line of argument lies in the meaning of extortion. While it may be quite correct that an extorted promise is no promise at all, it does not follow that consent to an unjust individual or organization is necessarily coerced. The analogy of a promise to an unjust person is instructive. It would be mistaken to suggest that a promise to an evil or unjust person results in no obligation to fulfill the promise. Rather, it is the strength of the obligation that can be mitigated or overridden by other (possibly) higher order moral considerations such as a duty to fight injustice. It becomes a matter of adjudicating the relative strength of the obligations and duties.

It may be objected that if the injustice of the institution to which you are ostensibly obligated is always a mitigating circumstance, then is not that the same as justice being a precondition of obligation?[164] Certainly, there may be individuals and organizations that are so thoroughly unjust that any obligation to them runs counter to the duty to fight injustice. This argument is sound, but is subtly different from Rawls's *ab initio* argument. The latter argument contains an intervening step in which the degree of injustice is weighed against the power of the obligation—the obligation is outweighed rather than immediately void. Such thorough evil and injustice are, moreover, thankfully rare. It is more typical that a given individual or organization is some mix of just and unjust. The question becomes how unjust an individual or organization has to be for all consent and obligations to them to be considered null and void. This brings the question back to that of adjudicating between the force of obligation and the degree of relevant injustice.

Some may suggest that the entire free-market system is unjust and therefore obligations within such a system are void. Although I do not believe this to be the case, a thorough critique or defense of the free-market system is outside the scope of the current inquiry. It is, moreover, at a different level of analysis than the project of establishing organization level moral obligations. I will simply assert that although certain aspects of free-market economies and specific organizations, in practice, create injustices, this does not serve as a blanket indictment of the entire free-market system nor less still of any particular organization within such a system. Even within the most egregiously unjust system, there may well be organizations and individuals that operate fairly. Obligations to these particular individuals and organizations are important considerations even when operating within an unjust system. Even when they are eventually overcome by other obligations or duties, they are still relevant to this determination.

Thus, if I voluntarily (i.e., uncoercedly) incur an obligation, then this obligation is relevant to moral decision making regardless of whether fulfillment of the obligation emerges as the most ethical course of action. While organizational or systemic injustice may override obligations, this does not render such obligations immediately void. Justice is relevant to obligations of fairness, but not a necessary precondition to such obligations at the individual or organizational level.

c. **Benefits that accrue only under conditions of near unanimity of cooperation** There are also strong reasons for doubting the necessity of this precondition for obligations of fairness. If all of the other necessary conditions obtain, it would still be unfair to take the benefits of a cooperative scheme without contribution, even if the benefits could be obtained under conditions of substantially less than unanimity of cooperation (i.e., the benefits could be obtained with only one-half or two-thirds of the people cooperating). Indeed, when the possibility of a great many free-riders exists, obligations of fairness take on an even greater significance.

Rawls includes the unanimity condition because the principle was originally suggested as a grounding for political obligations. In the current context, it is argued that the principle serves to create obligations in commercial interactions. As such, the unanimity condition may be a logical impossibility in this usage as the principle is designed to determine just who should or should not be included in the operative group. Therefore, the question, "unanimity among whom?" is suggested by this condition. If the particular group is unknown or undelimited, it is impossible to know how close the group is to unanimity. This was among the problems with using Rawls's "veil of ignorance" at the organizational level described in Chapter 3. Hence, this condition is discarded for current (organizational) uses.

d. **Cooperation that requires sacrifice or restriction of liberty on the part of participants**   In the case of the previous two conditions, I did not seek to determine whether commercial transactions qualified, because the two conditions were found unnecessary in the organizational context. Returning now to conditions of central importance to the idea of fairness, I also return to the effort of ascertaining the extent to which such conditions obtain in the sphere of commercial dealings. When a person engages in a trade, several restrictions on liberty arise. The most obvious example is that of the worker. When she agrees to sell the product of her labor to an organization, she generally must arrive at work on time, stay for a set period, and in general obey the rules and respect the norms of the organization. This clearly constitutes a restriction on the person's liberty.[165] So, too, is the case with the exchange of property. A property right is nothing more than a right to more or less exclusive use and thus in exchanging property, one actually sacrifices one's liberty to use that property.[166] Similarly, when a community allows a company to build a plant in its vicinity, it sacrifices its land and many other resources to the cooperative venture with the company, and the company sacrifices some of its capital assets as well. Commercial transactions involve sacrifice and restriction of liberty and thus meet this qualification as a cooperative scheme in which obligations of fairness may arise.

e. **The possibility of free-riders**   Given the breathtaking amount of research and literature on the problems of free-riders in commercial systems, it is difficult to conceive of what an argument against their existence would look like. I therefore take it as axiomatic that this condition is adequately met in the case of commercial transaction and interaction.[167]

f. **Voluntary acceptance of benefits of cooperative scheme** This condition is vital to the existence of obligations of fair play. It is the voluntary acceptance of the benefits of a scheme that actually create the obligations described. The voluntarist condition, one may notice, is not mentioned explicitly in the passage from the definition. It is, however, present in Rawls's definition in *Theory* and is vital to the relevance and viability of the principle.

It is axiomatic that uncoerced consent creates obligations on the part of the consenter and would provide adequate moral justification for such obligations. However, consent is not the only type of activity that may create such obligations. The voluntary engagement in, and acceptance of the benefits of, a cooperative scheme can similarly serve to create obligations of equal strength to the obligations created by consent. Such voluntary actions also provide strong normative justification for such obligations. In addition, such obligations based on fairness may be more useful than consent-based obligations due to the more frequent occurrence of the requisite obligation creating activity. Further, obligations of fairness exist even if the obligation creating implications of such activities are unknown to the actor. This is in contrast to consent-based theories wherein knowledge of the content of the obligation is imperative. Even express dissent cannot diminish the existence of obligations of fairness if the dissenter has undertaken the requisite acceptance of benefits from a cooperative scheme. The idea of voluntary acceptance will become clearer as I proceed.

The final attribute to the principle that is not explicit in Rawls's principle of fair play is nevertheless vital to the principle of stakeholder fairness. I call this the proportionality condition. As will become more evident during the defense of the principle, the obligation must be proportional with the benefit. Among the criticisms to be addressed is that nothing in the principle of fair play prevents one from being disproportionately obligated to a cooperative scheme while accepting relatively little of the benefit thereof. This is particularly important in the context of establishing obligations among organizations and their stakeholders.

Though there are several defensible schemes of distribution depending on the goals of the particular institution in question, organizations with commercial purposes and other private associations typically rely on merit or contribution as the appropriate scheme of distribution. As discussed in Chapter 3, the principle of stakeholder fairness is intended to apply to such private associations. Therefore, I have made explicit the idea that obligations are proportional to benefits.

I conclude on the basis of the previous discussion that commercial transactions do indeed qualify as cooperative schemes and, further, that these schemes admit of obligations of fairness. Therefore:

> Whenever persons or groups of persons voluntarily accept the benefits of a mutually beneficial scheme of co-operation requiring sacrifice or contribution on the parts of the participants and there exists the possibility of free-riding, obligations of fairness are created among the participants in the co-operative scheme in proportion to the benefits accepted.

As a caveat, it is logical that obligations of fair play would be reciprocal. Indeed, Rawls considered the concept of reciprocity central to his own work.[168] I will write mostly of the obligations owed by organizations to stakeholders; however, these obligations (nearly) always cut both ways. Where the firm has an obligation to a stakeholder group, the stakeholder group also has an obligation to the firm—although the strength and content of the obligations may vary. Further, inasmuch as the first qualification for the existence of such obligations is "mutual benefit," it follows that the obligations would also be reciprocal.

It might be objected at this point that the relationships described are legal and/or contractual ones and that little or nothing is added through allusion to stakeholder obligations. That there is a vast amount of regulation, legislation, and legal precedent attendant to the relationships between organizations and stakeholders is conceded. This does not lead to the conclusion that stakeholder obligations are redundant or meaningless. In fact, fairness-based stakeholder obligations may be the normative motivation for much of this law, though I shall not attempt to argue for this here. Contracts are notoriously incomplete. Employment contracts cannot possibly state in advance every duty of an employee, even at the lowest levels of the organization. Some stakeholder relationships are not the subject of formal contracts. Many small transactions with customers do not require contracts. Nor are the organization's obligations to local communities always the subject of a formal contracting process. The concept of noncontractual relationships with derivatively legitimate stakeholders (i.e., stakeholders whose status is derived from their power to affect others for good or ill) is discussed in the next chapter.

In addition to independent standing as moral obligations alongside contracts, fairness-based moral obligations to stakeholders may be considered interstitial. They fill in the gaps left underdetermined by the legal system. These are moral obligations that add richness and detail to the thin, formal relationships established in contracts and other legislation and regulation. While the legal system dictates much about stakeholder relations, there is still much left to the moral discretion of managers and administrators. The principle of stakeholder fairness provides a moral basis for directing this discretion.

Obligations

A vital feature of the principle of stakeholder fairness is the technical meaning of the term *obligation*. As such, it is important to note what is meant by obligation in the current context and how obligations are different from other moral concepts such as *duty*. This distinction is vital to the two-tiered approach necessary to organizational ethics discussed in Chapter 3.

Obligation, as the term is used here and following Hart, Rawls, and Simmons,[169] carries a somewhat technical meaning. An obligation is characterized by four conditions:

1. An obligation is a moral requirement generated by the performance of some voluntary act (or omission).
2. An obligation is owed by a specific person (the "obligor") to a specific person or persons (the "obligee[s]").
3. For every obligation generated, a correlative right is simultaneously generated.
4. It is the nature of the transaction or relationships into which the obligor and obligee enter, not the nature of the required act, which renders the act obligatory.

Taken in order, the first condition is vital in discussions of stakeholder theory because stakeholder status, if it is to be meaningful, must indicate some degree of *additional* moral consideration from the organization and its managers over and above that due all humans *as* humans. This additional moral consideration arises from the voluntary, obligation-generating act of cooperatively creating and accepting benefits or goods of some kind.

The voluntary omission in the first condition refers to, for example, the failure to speak under conditions where one's silence indicates consent. A meeting where the leader says, "We will meet Monday at 5:00 unless there are objections," is an occasion when silence or omission means having consented to the meeting and having created an obligation to be there.

The second condition (an obligation is owed by a specific person to a specific person or persons), similar to the first condition, indicates that an obligation implies a specificity of the parties involved as opposed to a duty that is due all. Both the first and second conditions can be contrasted with "duties," which are owed by all to all simply by virtue of being human. In the case of obligations, however, specifiable acts create the obligations and specific parties to the obligations.

This second condition should not be misunderstood as a requirement of methodological individualism. That is, it should not be read as excluding collective entities from being either obligors or obligees. The "specific person or persons" conditions is to be contrasted with the "all people" nature of duties rather than with "groups of people."

The third condition is rather straightforward. The creation of an obligation also creates a right on the part of the obligee to fulfill the obligation. Rights are also, however, correlative with duties owed to all (e.g., human rights). As such, to avoid confusion of this and other sorts, this book will have little discussion of rights.

Lastly, the existence or nonexistence of obligations is not based on content of the obligation, but the obligating act itself. For example, I am under no obligation to not murder you (although I obviously have a duty to not murder you and you have a right not to be murdered) unless I state, "I hereby promise to not murder you," at which point I incur the obligation. Note that it is not the nature of the act of murdering that created the obligation, but the nature of the act of promising.

The preceding discussion of the nature of obligations is important for two closely related reasons. First, the distinction between obligations and duties described by the first two conditions help to respond to the problem of stakeholder identity—the problem raised and exemplified by the discussion in Chapter 7 of the stakeholder status of the natural environment. Secondly, obligations of the type described provide the backbone for a fairness-based stakeholder framework from which claims of stakeholder status for the natural environment will be analyzed. It is to the fairness-based approach that I shall now return for a description of those parts of the model that bear on the current topic.

Summarizing the arguments to this point, I have argued that an amended principle of fairness that I call the principle of stakeholder fairness is operative in all contexts of commercial interaction. Hence, obligations of fairness exist between and among an organization and its stakeholders. The principle of stakeholder fairness thereby provides a normative justificatory framework for stakeholder theory. In the next section I discuss some objections to the principle and compare the fairness-based stakeholder framework to another justly well-known theory of organizational ethics. In the process I hope to further clarify the principle and its operation as well as suggest some theoretical advantages that it may hold over other theories.

Defending Fairness

While many have criticized the principle of fairness as a grounds for the political obligation for which it was originally intended,[170] Robert Nozick argues that it fails as a moral principle in every context.[171] His arguments are answerable with the addition of the voluntary acceptance condition and the distinctions it makes possible. Nozick begins with the following example of his interpretation of the principle of fairness:

> Suppose some of the people in your neighborhood (there are 364 adults) have found a public address system and decide to institute a system of public entertainment. They post a list of names, one for each day, yours among them. On his assigned day (one can easily switch days) a person is to run the public address system, play records over it, give news bulletins, tell amusing stories he has heard and so on. After 138 days on which each person has done his part, your day arrives. Are you obligated to take a turn? You have benefited from it, occasionally opening your window to listen, enjoying some music or chuckling at someone's funny story. The other people have put themselves out. But

must you answer the call when it is your turn to do so? As it stands, surely not. Though you benefit from the arrangement, you may know all along that 364 days of entertainment supplied by others will not be worth your giving up one day . . . Whatever you want, can others create obligations for you to do so by going ahead and starting the program themselves? . . .

At the very least one wants to build into the principle of fairness the condition that the benefits to a person from the actions of others are greater than the cost to him of doing his share.[172]

Nozick uses this and another example of people who thrust books into your living room and subsequently demand payment for the books as arguments against the principle of fairness. Nozick's examples suffer, however, from a serious misinterpretation and confusion concerning the operation of the principle. In these examples, the person Nozick finds exempt from obligations of fairness may indeed be exempt from such obligations (or subject only to a lesser degree than others). But it is not due to the failure of the principle in general, but rather to Nozick's conflation of voluntary acceptance and mere receipt of benefits. In the cases he cites, the relevant people are, to use Simmons's phrase, "innocent bystanders" and not members of the cooperative scheme in the appropriate sense.

In the examples described, the scheme has been built up around the person in question making the person, therefore, not a party to the scheme in the appropriate sense. The person has not acted in such a way as to be interpreted as having voluntarily accepted the benefits in question. The person neither tried to get (and succeeded in getting) the benefit nor took the benefit willingly and knowingly.[173] Instead, the person has merely received the benefit of others' sacrifice through no action of his own. In such a case a person indeed has no special obligation of fairness vis-à-vis the particular scheme in question; this does not, however, tell against the principle in general, because the example is based on a misunderstanding of the principle and its conditions.

It would not, however, be entirely accurate to say that the person in the PA system example has no obligations. Recall that Nozick says, "You have benefited from it, occasionally opening your window to listen, enjoying some music or chuckling at someone's funny story." Arguably, this activity—opening the window and enjoying—may indeed create obligations of fairness on that person's part. The obligations may not be of the same magnitude or content as the obligations that the organizers and real PA aficionados hold by virtue of these latter receiving greater benefit from the scheme; but obligations exist nonetheless. Thus, while some people may be obligated to give more than one day, the person in the example may only be required to contribute several hours to the scheme with the content of the obligation based on the benefit received. This is consistent with the equitable proportionality and meritocracy condition in the principle of stakeholder fairness.

Finally, Nozick ends his treatment of the fairness principle by stating:

> Hence, even if the principle could be formulated so that it was no longer open to objection, it would not serve to obviate the need for other persons' consenting to cooperate and limit their own activities.[174]

Nozick is here expressing the idea that obligations based on fairness devolve into or require some form of consent and thus offer nothing new in moral theory. In a later section I will contrast obligations of fairness with consent-based obligations—to show that Nozick is mistaken on this last count. The principle of fairness is indeed different from consent and creates obligations that are no less binding than those based on such consent. In fact, I will show that obligations of fairness may render consent redundant in some cases.

To summarize, objections to the principle of fairness such as those of Nozick are based on a misunderstanding of the principle itself. Nozick's "innocent bystander" objections do not take proper account of the volitionality condition of the fairness principle and therefore do not count against it. It is the fact that the benefits are *voluntarily* accepted that renders the obligation.

Fairness and Consent

Scholars of both political theory and organizational ethics have attempted to account for the obligations of individuals and associations, respectively, through the use of what they term "tacit" or "implicit" consent. There is, of course, some reason for the initial belief that obligations of fairness are the same as actual or tacit consent. For one thing, many of the situations that would ordinarily give rise to obligations of fairness are also often characterized by a consensual relationship. This would be the case especially at the inception of a given cooperative scheme wherein it is the original cooperators who initiate, participate in, and gain the benefits of the scheme. In cases such as these, characterized by actual mutual consent, obligations of fairness would indeed be redundant and superfluous although extant nonetheless. However, obligations do arise within cooperative schemes quite apart from consent. In fact, obligations of fairness may exist even in the face of express dissent if the person or group in question does indeed successfully and voluntarily undertake to receive the benefits of the scheme.

An example may help clarify the difference between the principle of fairness and consent. Suppose that workers in an office agree that they all enjoy coffee, tea, and small snacks and wish to establish a breakfast club. Each person is expected to contribute a set amount to the venture each week for the purchase of the necessary goods. At the beginning of the breakfast club, those who wish to join the venture consent to become members and to contribute their share. Further, after some time others may wish to join the breakfast club, thus consenting to future contributions. All the people to this point have obligations based both on consent and fairness to do their share. However, we may further suppose that there is a person in the office who is a known coffee lover who, though invited, declined to join the breakfast club at its inception saying, "This is a ridiculous idea and I will never consent to such a scheme." Once the venture was successfully underway, however, she is often seen taking coffee and occasionally a doughnut. She is even overheard walking down the hall shouting, "You people needn't think that this means I'm consenting to your scheme. I still think the idea of a breakfast club is absurd and I'll not join in." This person clearly refuses to consent, but does she not still incur obligations to the scheme? Despite the absence of an act of consent, she has engaged in a voluntary action that creates equally strong obligations based on the principle of fairness.

Some may still wish to argue that the activity requisite for the creation of obligations of fairness (e.g., taking the coffee from the co-op) amounts to nothing more than tacit or implicit consent. That is, by partaking of the benefits of the scheme one has tacitly or implicitly consented to doing her part in the scheme and, therefore, the obligations of fairness remain nothing more than a special kind of consent. This is the stance taken in recent work by Donaldson and Dunfee on their Integrative Social Contracts Theory (ISCT). The next section further clarifies the conception of tacit consent and other pertinent issues raised by Donaldson and Dunfee's important work.

Fairness and Integrative Social Contracts Theory

In two essays and a book, Donaldson and Dunfee describe and defend their ISCT.[175] In addition to helping us better understand the preceding discussion of tacit consent, ISCT also contains many other points of interest for comparison with the fairness model and therefore merits a rather close inspection in the current context. This section will consist of a brief summary of ISCT, a brief critique of the idea of tacit consent in ISCT, and an analysis of Donaldson and Dunfee's treatment of the principle of fairness.

ISCT   ISCT is a two-tier hypothetical social contract conception for the modeling of organizational and commercial morality. On this account, there is first a macro social contract that binds for all people in all societies. This macro social contract is similar to many others in that it should describe what people in a suitable initial situation such as Rawls's original position would rationally agree to. This much is standard social contract theory.

Donaldson and Dunfee go on to describe their micro social contract that they take to be communitarian in nature. That is, the macro social contractors will insist on "moral free space" in their commercial (and presumably other private) dealings and as such will allow some latitude in the establishment of ethical criteria within the myriad commercial and other communities. The more specific agreements concerning the ethics of these various communities are the subject matter of the micro social contracts. The ethical norms dictated by the micro social contracts are, however, subject to their compatibility with the "hypernorms" of the macro contract as well as being subject to various priority rules for arbitrating between community norms.

Although the fairness theory discussed here has several commonalties with ISCT, they differ importantly regarding the source of moral obligations. ISCT relies heavily on the idea of tacit consent and an examination of this concept is vital to illuminate the difference between the two theories.

Tacit Consent   Donaldson and Dunfee are not insensitive to the objections that have been raised regarding tacit consent.

> Consent to membership in a community can derive from an express contractual commitment as in the case of entering into an employment contract with a term of years, or it may just involve participating in a group. . . . Consent may thus be found in an express commitment to membership in a community, but it may also be implied from an individual's actions in participating in a community. . . . In many instances, one may

implicitly consent to membership by making instrumental use of a community.[176]

In political theory, tacit consent has been severely criticized as a basis for political obligation, as has reliance upon attitudinal factors in finding tacit consent (Simmons, 1979, generally at p. 93). . . . Indeed, reliance upon attitudinal factors in discussing norms and conventions is supported by the literature.[177]

The criticisms to which they refer hinge on the distinction between acts that are "signs of consent" and acts that "imply consent."[178] Acts that can be taken as "signs of consent" constitute actual express consent, but are not restricted to positive action. Thus, actions such as the statement, "I consent to be a part of scheme X" may be considered a sign of consent as may silence in the appropriate context. For instance, when the person presiding over a wedding asks, "Is there anyone here who objects to this marriage?" then silence in this context would be a sign of consent. Tacit in the sense of "signs of consent" refers to how the consent is expressed rather than the absence of expression. Donaldson and Dunfee are after something like the example of "silence as consent" in the note on fairness that will be discussed shortly.

Acts that imply consent, on the other hand, are actually no consent at all. Rather, they may be either acts that demonstrate a favorable attitude toward the prospect in question or acts that induce obligations similar to those induced by genuine express consent (e.g., obligations of fairness). The attitudinal form of consent involves actions that lead one to believe that, were the appropriate conditions to obtain, the actor would (or would have) indeed consent(ed). Donaldson and Dunfee write:

> [W]hen there is a question concerning whether an action implies consent, it is appropriate to use further means, such as scientific surveys of *attitudes*, to determine whether consent is genuine. . . .

Under ISCT, *the ultimate test is whether or not one has sufficient association with a community to allow for an attribution of moral obligation.* This may be based on a formal, contractual connection, but it may also be based on entering into a transaction environment in which one acts within the boundaries of a self-recognized group and participates to fulfill some particular desire.... It might be the case, for example, that a community might excuse the elderly or infirm from certain obligations of membership, effectively on the grounds that there is insufficient reason to *assume* consent to authentic norm obligations (emphasis added).[179]

No genuine act of consent has been performed under these circumstances. Rather it is the opinions and conclusions of others that dictate that the actor has obligated herself. This is contrary to the Hart/Rawls/Simmons understanding of "obligation" employed here according to which a voluntary action by the obligated entity is required. Consent is not something that others *assume* for us based on our attitudes.

This attitude-based implied consent runs afoul of Nozick's "book thrusting" example. One may enjoy the books thrown into her living room, she may even appreciate the delivery service, but there is no obligation generated to pay for the books. One must perform some action or appropriate omission to be obligated, rather than have an obligation imputed by a survey. Actual consent is such an act, but barring that, Donaldson and Dunfee require something like the principle of fairness to generate an obligation. They come close to the principle of stakeholder fairness in describing "the ultimate test" for ISCT: "[S]ufficient association" sounds much closer to a fairness-based obligation than a consent-based one. I briefly compare the implied consent of ISCT with fairness-based obligations in this chapter.

Donaldson and Dunfee's final defense against these arguments over tacit consent is that of minimizing the importance of the distinction between actual and tacit consent.

> The original macro contractors who rely upon consent are not
> seeking to justify coercive power on the part of the state, or the
> imposition of severe punishments. Instead they are concerned with
> ethical standards in business; normative principles whose enforce-
> ment will be through informal sanctions and mechanisms.[180]

But, the commercial sphere of life in the early twenty-first century is every bit as important as the political if not more so as
multinational corporations extend beyond any geopolitical
boundaries. Indeed, the current political environment is often
driven by considerations of a commercial nature. Further, it is
unclear how the relative importance of the context in which
obligations arise has any bearing on which type of actions constitute express consent, which create obligations of other
kinds, and which create no obligations at all.

Employing a similar strategy, they write: "In most of the basic
cases of business ethics, we do not believe that this issue of consent to membership is a serious problem. Employees are bound
by legitimate corporate morality. . ."[181] How employees come to
be so bound is precisely the question at issue. The repeated
response of minimizing the relevance of consent is a dubious
one—especially in light of the centrality of consent to the overall project of ISCT (according to the index, *consent* appears over
forty times under eight different headings in *Ties That Bind*).

ISCT and Fairness   Although the evidence of it lies in a
note, Donaldson and Dunfee are aware of the possibility of
obligations of fairness.

> Fair play has been recognized as a supplemental justification for
> obligation in political theory and in law (Greenawalt, 1989) and,
> particularly in the context of ethics in economic life, it can repre-
> sent an important justification for basing obligation on consent to
> membership, buttressed by a right of exit. We assume that the par-
> ticipants in the macro social contract are willing to allow for con-
> sent to norms to be implied when individuals are making instru-

mental use of economic institutions. Therefore, the macro social contract announces in advance the circumstances under which consent will be implied. Such an approach combines fairness with a notice-based approach to consent. Individuals are given advance notice that consent will be assumed in certain circumstances. Therefore, if they act in a manner in which they know that consent will be inferred, they are held to have consented.[182]

Although several points of interest here have already been covered, I will briefly mention then again. First, consistent with the conflation of acts that imply consent and acts that are signs of consent, they see fairness as merely a kind of consent ("it can represent an important justification for basing obligation on consent to membership"). Second, there is an attempt alluded to earlier to bring what are clearly acts that imply consent closer to the type of acts that are seen as signs of consent (and therefore qualify as true consent). This is the effect of the "notice-based approach to consent" and is analogous to the example of the wedding where silence can be taken as an expression of consent within the appropriate background context. Such a move would bring the theory more in line with a genuine consent theory.

A third point of interest in this passage concerns the use of the word are in the passage reading, "Individuals are given advance notice that consent will be assumed in certain circumstances." The sentence appears to be descriptive in nature; that is, it looks to be depicting an actual activity in organizational contexts that would thus bolster the claims to tacit consent. However, such an activity is observed rarely at best in such situations. The quoted passage is not a description of actual economic or organizational experiences.

Another alternative is that the passage is normative and thus indicates how the world would or should operate according to the ISCT contracts. However, if the fairness model described herein holds, then the requirement that people be given advance notice is unnecessary in establishing moral obligation in organizational and commercial contexts and may be redundant in most cases. This brings us to the final and most interesting point from this passage.

Whereas Nozick, and to some extent Donaldson and Dunfee, wish to reduce obligations of fairness into obligations of consent, thus rendering the former redundant, the quoted passage shows how the opposite is often the case in such theories. If a person is engaged in a cooperative scheme under the circumstances of the "notice-based approach to consent" and they are voluntarily receiving the benefits of the scheme, then there already exist obligations of fairness. In this situation, the inaction and the consent for which it is taken as a sign after due notice is itself redundant. What is added to the obligation of fairness that already exists when the person's notice is up and she is taken to have consented? Consent adds nothing to the extant obligations of fairness in such cases. In addition to the possibility that obligations of fairness may be rendered meaningless in some circumstances by preexisting consent-based obligations, so too the opposite may be true. It seems to be a matter of temporal priority, which is to be deemed operative. Or, as is more likely the case, it may be a matter of factual occurrence. In the actual world of transactions and economic cooperative schemes, there may be many fewer incidents of genuine consent than Donaldson and Dunfee require to make their theory adequately general. Alternatively, as argued earlier, virtually any commercial transaction may be interpreted as a cooperative scheme.

I have argued that the principle of fairness, properly conceived, does not fall victim to Nozick's criticisms. Neither do obligations of fairness depend on nor devolve into a form of consent. Indeed, obligations of stakeholder fairness have an advantage over such tacit consent-based theories as ISCT—the obligation-generating activities of the principle of stakeholder fairness actually happen in concrete situations.

It has been suggested, however, that the principle of stakeholder fairness is not adequately Foundational to provide the justification so claimed. The next section addresses this criticism.

On the Question of Justification

Among the primary goals of the fairness-based stakeholder theory suggested here is the provision of a normative justification for stakeholder theory; for want of which the model has been justly criticized. Some, however, have criticized the fairness-based model as itself being little better than extant stakeholder literature on this point; that is, the principle of stakeholder fairness provides little more normative justification of the necessary type than any other discussion of the model.

As I understand the criticism, the fairness-based model does not qualify as a normative foundation because it is inadequately "Foundational." The principle of stakeholder fairness makes no reference to any "comprehensive moral theory."

There are at least two ways to answer this criticism. First is the pragmatist line. While I will not attempt to address all of the myriad intricacies of the pragmatist critique of metaphysics and foundationalism, I would like to express a level of skepticism regarding the existence of a Foundational Truth. Various stories allow humans to live. Some stories allow us to live better, some worse. Some narratives are more convincing than others and some less. Scientific explanations, for example, receive a great deal of credence in modern society—and for good reason. The methods of science have yielded society an unprecedented level of material comfort for much of the world.

However, our success in discovering more and more about our world and ourselves has created a false sense of comfort in our abilities to discover the Truth. There is no better reason to believe that we are now in possession of the Truth any more than were the well-informed of the time of Ptolemy[183] or Kant. In short, my initial response to the critic's charge that the principle of stakeholder fairness provides no Foundation is that there is no such Foundation to provide. As with Descartes's "evil genie" objection (see Chapter 2), this criticism counts no more against the principle of stakeholder fairness than any other theory.[184] The principle of stakeholder fairness is a deeper justification than is currently available in the literature and as such represents an advance in our understanding of stakeholder theory. For current purposes, it is as deep as I will be attempting to delve. I have every reason to believe, however, that still deeper explications and justifications exist and will be the subject of later exploration.

The second response to the critique that the principle of stakeholder fairness does not count as justification of the required kind is to point out that it provides an amendment and addition to Rawls's *Theory of Justice*. Elaboration on the principle of fairness is an attempt to describe what a Rawlsian conception of the organizational organization might look like.

Various scholars have attempted to describe what could be termed a Rawlsian view of the organization. They have searched for answers to the question, What would the organization look like within a Rawlsian framework?[185] Their explications, however, relied heavily on the use of the Rawlsian "veil of ignorance." What made the particular theory "Rawlsian" was the suggestion that its parameters be established in some original position where the relevant stakeholders are ignorant of their place in the organization once the veil of ignorance is lifted. (I am sympathetic to such models having worked for some time on a similar such model).

As discussed in Chapter 3, Rawls explicitly does not intend that his use of the original position extend to "private associations." Although the economic system as a whole is clearly within the purview of the original position, individual corporations are not. For this and other reasons described in Chapter 3, I argue that something like the principle of stakeholder fairness is more consistent with Rawls's justice as fairness than is the use of the veil of ignorance in the description of the Rawlsian organization.

This argument has implications for the foundationalist critic: If one seeks a deeper justification for the principle of stakeholder fairness, then Rawls's justice as fairness provides such a justification. The principle of stakeholder fairness is an elaboration and expansion of Rawls's theory and represents the conception of the private association most consistent with a Rawlsian framework.

Rawls himself is an antifoundationalist of a sort and so the two responses to the foundationalist critique may still not satisfy the critic's objection. Inasmuch as Rawls defends himself far better than ever I could, I defer to his arguments for his own framework and submit that, for those who would demand a deeper justification than is here provided, justice as fairness provides such depth.

Discourse Ethics and the Content of Stakeholder Obligations

As mentioned previously, the principle of stakeholder fairness provides only the method for deriving stakeholder obligations— the principle itself provides no content to the obligations. In other words, the principle of stakeholder fairness determines that there are obligations, but not what the parties are obligated to do. As such, the principle of stakeholder fairness might be criticized as inadequately practical or even hollow—the whole enterprise an exercise in empty formalism. This criticism is partially correct. The principle of stakeholder fairness by itself is indeed unable to direct a manager's action. This is not, however, what the principle is intended to do. Rather, the principle describes how obligations arise among stakeholders. The content of the obligations arises within the specific context of the stakeholders' interactions. The stakeholders decide among themselves how the cooperative scheme is to be organized once it is determined who are the participants.

Rather than taking any norm to be as good as any other, stakeholder norms in particular contexts may be critically analyzed using the method of communicative (discourse) ethics. The work of Jürgen Habermas is among the most interesting, thorough, and insightful in the literature on discourse ethics. I will briefly discuss Habermas's work as a potential contribution to stakeholder thought and practice. The following is at best suggestive of an outline of Habermas's work and is farther still from representing a serious contribution to the literature on discourse ethics. The idea is merely to point out the relationship between actual organizational norms and the principle of stakeholder fairness as well as hint at a possible source of adjudicating disagreements among competing stakeholder norms.

Habermas defends and explicates a particular methodology for justifying moral norms called discourse (or communicative) ethics. He argues for the following principle of discourse ethics.

> (D) Only those norms can claim to be valid that meet (or could meet) with the approval of all affected in their capacity *as participants in a practical discourse.*[186]

Consistent with the way in which the method of discourse ethics is used here, Habermas's (D) provides a means of *testing* moral norms rather than *generating* them. It is thus, at one level at least, able to answer the neo-Hegelian and postmodern criticisms of formalistic ethics in general. These criticisms argue, in general, that any theory that attempts a foundational, ahistorical, transcendent justification of ethics is undertaken in vain due to the impossibility of escaping our own embeddedness in a particular culture and language. Habermas suggests that discourse ethics is able to avoid this problem because it is not formal in the sense criticized. Rather than generating justified moral norms, discourse ethics serves as a means for testing the validity of already extant societal norms. As such it depends on the existence of real norms and real conflict between norms for its content. Discourse ethics is more in touch with the "historical facticity" of the discussants and the neo-Hegelian critique is thus diminished.

Habermas goes on to distinguish between strategic and communicative action. Whereas the latter is a moral activity, the former does not so qualify.

> Whereas in strategic action one actor seeks to *influence* the behavior of another by means of the threat of sanctions or the prospect of gratification in order to *cause* the interaction to continue as the first actor desires, in communicative action one actor seeks *rationally* to *motivate* another by relying on the illocutionary binding/bonding effect (*Bindungseffekt*) of the offer contained in his speech act.[187]

Inasmuch as the principle of stakeholder fairness is a moral principle, the method of discourse employed in testing the validity of the content of the obligations generated by the principle must also be moral. In other words, the discourse by which stakeholder norms are tested must have moral (i.e., communicative) restrictions rather than being merely strategic in nature.

For discourse ethics, these restrictions consist in what Habermas calls an "ideal speech situation" wherein "all external or internal coercion other than the force of the better argument" is ruled out. Thus, for example, a stakeholder discourse in which threats of layoffs are employed by management or strikes by labor unions *as a strategic ploy* would be considered strategic in character and not communicative and therefore not moral. Similarly, an organization that employs strong-arm tactics on its suppliers to try and force their prices lower would be in conflict with the aims of the ideal speech situation. A communicative discourse would, rather, attempt to establish norms that would be in the best interest of the cooperative scheme and

would best conduce to the continuation of that scheme of cooperation and, in this way, may qualify as a moral stakeholder discourse. While difficult in practice, the implication is that managing for stakeholders would entail duplicating as far as possible
the conditions of the ideal speech situation.

Ed Freeman describes a time when he was called to consult
a large organization on stakeholder management. He was
taken into a room that "looked like mission control" filled with
elaborate stakeholder maps, flow charts and computers. After
surveying the contents of the room, Freeman asks, "How many
stakeholders have you spoken with?" The answer was something like, "Well none. We've been too busy making stakeholder maps and flow charts."[188]

Such is the problem that is better addressed using a Haber-
masian ethic of discourse. Whereas many managers would be
content to attempt to adjudicate between myriad stakeholders
in the comfort of their own offices, such a method relies only on
the individual manager's perceptions of who the stakeholders
are and what they would like to gain from their cooperation
with the organization.[189] Frequently managers use internal
proxies for determining stakeholder interests. For example,
they rely on personnel or human resources departments for
information regarding employee concerns, the marketing or
sales department provides a proxy for the interests of customers,
corporate finance is relied on for financier interests; and public
relations is used to ascertain community interests. The discourse
ethic described here eschews such approaches in favor of direct
contact between managers and stakeholders. Actual discourse
with the various stakeholders gives a more accurate representation of what the stakeholders want and hence provides the manager with better information on which to base a decision. Work
is just beginning on a discursive methodology in organizational
ethics by, for example, Jerry Calton[190] and Richard Nielson.[191]

An interesting example of a company that seems to exemplify stakeholder discursive management is Cadbury's.[192] This

company was founded upon "a belief in achieving, as far as one can, agreement by consensus." This belief enabled Cadbury's to withstand the growing hostility between labor and the Conservative Party (e.g., under Margaret Thatcher) in Great Britain.

Cadbury's faced a situation that called for an updating of the company's tea packaging equipment. The equipment upgrade also meant, however, that the work that had been previously undertaken in two packaging plants would now require only one plant and fewer workers. Rather than simply a "hard-nosed business decision," Adrian Cadbury viewed the decision through a stakeholder lens.

> The . . . aspect of ethics in business decisions I want to discuss concerns our responsibility for the level of employment; what can or should companies do about the provision of jobs? . . . The company's prime responsibility to everyone who has a stake in it is to retain its competitive edge, even if this means a loss of jobs in the short run. Where companies do have a social responsibility, however, is in how we manage this situation, how we smooth the path of technological change. Companies are responsible for the timing of such changes and we are in a position to involve those who will be affected by the way in which those changes are introduced.[193]

This way of viewing a difficult situation is consistent with the fairness-based stakeholder theory sketched here. Cadbury's (the company) and Adrian Cadbury himself exhibit a long-standing commitment to a concern for stakeholder well-being.

To solve the problem, Cadbury's formed a "working party" (such problem-solving groups were a part of Cadbury's tradition consistent with the previous statements) including managers, engineers, and shop stewards from both tea packaging plants. The solution of the working party—by unanimous consent—was to close one of the plants and operate with only half the workers. The decision also included "a package of employment displacement benefits with intraorganizational transfers, preferential rehiring, and layoff benefits . . ."[194] This decision could have been (and indeed has been) made in a more autocratic, top-down way with the same outcomes; however, the stakeholder discursive method of management tends away from the kinds of animosity and distrust that often characterize nearly identical decisions in such difficult situations.

Therefore, if the situation is one in which management chooses to fire workers merely to *increase the profits* to the financiers, then it violates the principle of stakeholder fairness, because it privileges one stakeholder group (the share owners) to the detriment of another vital stakeholder group (the employees). Further, this norm is unlikely to meet with the communicative assent of all stakeholders. Employees would not agree to a norm stipulating that employees be fired in order merely to improve profits under the conditions of an ideal speech situation. The absence (impossibility) of a reasonable consensus denies the discursive validity of that norm.

However, the case may be otherwise if the layoffs are to preclude the dissipation of the organization itself. That is, if some layoffs are necessary to save the bulk of the jobs and other benefits derived by other stakeholder groups, then this action may more readily meet with agreement among stakeholders (including the employees). In this case, one stakeholder group is not being privileged at the expense of another stakeholder group; rather, the layoffs are for the sake of the continuation of the cooperative scheme itself and *may*, therefore, meet with agreement among all stakeholder groups. Such appears to be the case for Cadbury's.

Cadbury's tradition of stakeholder management is not exclusive to employees, however.

> Starting with the assumption that Capital and Labour, Management and Workers, Manufacturers and Distributors, are to be collaborators in the enterprise of serving the community, it is worth while trying to determine the sort of industrial organisation which can pursue this aim most effectively.[195]

As stated here, Cadbury's bears a striking similarity to Freeman's notion that stakeholders are analytic to business organizations. Cadbury's simply starts with the assumption that these constituencies are indispensable to the operations of the organization. Stakeholder obligations do not require further defense for Cadbury. This "analytic justification" merits a brief discussion.

Stakeholders as Analytic to Business

In logic, something is said to be *analytic* when it necessarily follows from some previous concept—a tautology. It has been argued that the principle of stakeholder fairness is unnecessary because stakeholders are analytic to business and organizations. Stakeholder theory does not require such a justification because business organizations are incomprehensible without stakeholders. All business organizations have consumers of their outputs, providers of inputs and creators of value, financiers, and a social context within which these myriad interactions take place. The concept of the business organization is dependent on the contributions of these groups and it could not exist without them. Discussion of organizations simply implies stakeholders; the moral status of stakeholders is in need of no further justification.

This analytic justification of stakeholders recalls the 1963 Stanford Research Institute memo defining stakeholders as "those groups without whose support the organization would cease to exist."[196] This definition may be read as a conditional empirical statement. Should one of these groups withdraw its support for the organization, the organization itself would no longer be viable and would disintegrate. However, this definition may also be interpreted as a requirement of conceptual coherence. Not only would a business organization fail (empirically and strategically) as a going concern should a stakeholder withdraw its support, but also it could no longer be (conceptually) considered a business organization at all. According to the analytic justification, without stakeholders, there is no business organization at all.

Though a reasonable and popular approach, and one that would have great practitioner appeal, the analytic justification of stakeholder theory could be considered preaching to the choir. Certainly these groups are necessary to the functioning, or even conceptual coherence, of the business organization, but it could be argued that this does not necessarily entail an obligation to them. For those who, like Cadbury, believe that doing business assumes an obligation to stakeholders, the principle of stakeholder fairness may add little. For those for whom stakeholder obligations do require further justification, the principle of stakeholder fairness provides such underpinning.

Conclusion

This chapter discusses the Rawls/Hart principle of fair play (including a suggestion that the principle has a heritage at least back to Mill) and the principle of stakeholder fairness on which it is based. Rawls argues that the principle of fairness is the appropriate method by which to establish obligations among less than basic structure entities within his "justice as fairness" framework. This chapter analyzes Rawls's principle of fair play and suggests the following principle of stakeholder fairness for organizational contexts.

> Whenever persons or groups of persons voluntarily accept the benefits of a mutually beneficial scheme of co-operation requiring sacrifice or contribution on the parts of the participants and there exists the possibility of free-riding, obligations of fairness are created among the participants in the co-operative scheme in proportion to the benefits accepted.

This principle suggests how obligations among organizational stakeholders arise.

The distinction between obligations, rights, and duties was also elaborated. The principle of stakeholder fairness creates obligations among the stakeholders distinct from the duties that these individuals and groups may have with regard to one another by virtue of their humanity.

As a means of further explicating the principle of stakeholder fairness, this chapter defends the principle against the criticisms that have been leveled against it by, for example, Nozick in *Anarchy, State, and Utopia*. Nozick conflates the ideas of voluntary acceptance and mere receipt of benefits. It is argued that once this difference between the two is accounted for, Nozick's critique is nugatory.

After defending the principle against Nozick's critique and by way of further explication, I contrast the principle of stakeholder fairness with Donaldson and Dunfee's Integrative Social Contracts Theory. This comparison allowed for further discussion of the important distinction between obligations of fairness and tacit consent. ISCT leans heavily on the idea of tacit consent. It is argued that tacit consent amounts to no consent at all and that the obligations described in ISCT may instead bear resemblance to obligations of stakeholder fairness. It is further argued that the principle of stakeholder fairness is a more useful description of organizational obligations than even actual consent in many organizational contexts due to the more frequent occurrence of the obligation-generating activity.

A final point is the difference between the establishment of obligations of stakeholder fairness and the content of the obligations. The principle of stakeholder fairness only provides for the existence of obligations among stakeholders; the content of the obligations is established and tested within the particular contexts of organizational interaction. That there are obligations and who the parties to these obligations are is determined using the principle of stakeholder fairness, while the content of these obligations (i.e., what the parties are obligated to do or refrain from doing) is established by the norms of the particular organization and its stakeholders.

It is not the case, however, that *any* norms are acceptable. Agreement while facing the business end of a revolver does not establish a legitimate norm. Coercion does exist and it does impact the moral validity of extant norms. A method is needed by which to test stakeholder norms. The method of discourse ethics is suggested and elaborated as a candidate for testing extant organizational norms.

This chapter has undertaken to elaborate what stakeholder theory is and what moral concepts underlie stakeholder status and organizational obligations to constituency groups. In the course of this elaboration, I defend the principle of fair play against actual and potential criticism. Having done so, the next chapters defend a version of stakeholder theory based on the principle of stakeholder fairness. The first concept is that of stakeholder legitimacy in light of this principle.

CHAPTER 6

Stakeholder Legitimacy

*Stakeholder theory should not be used to weave a basket big
enough to hold the world's misery.*

— MAX CLARKSON[197]

It was argued at the beginning of this project that one of the
theoretical shortcomings of previous stakeholder scholarship is the problem of stakeholder identity.[198] For reasons to
be adduced in this chapter, this problem may be attributed to
a poor understanding of the concept of legitimacy in stakeholder theory. In this and the following chapter I will elaborate on how the problem of stakeholder legitimacy may be
remedied using the principle of stakeholder fairness. Rather
than merely stakeholders and nonstakeholders, the category
of stakeholder should be further subdivided into normative
stakeholders and derivative stakeholders (following the Donaldson and Preston taxonomy) with only the former being
entitled to fairness-based stakeholder consideration.

Legitimacy in Stakeholder Theory

Stakeholder legitimacy has been a central concern at least since Freeman's groundbreaking discussion. Though concerned with questions of legitimacy, Freeman chose to "put aside" such matters.

> "Stakeholder" connotes "legitimacy," and while managers may not think that certain groups are "legitimate" in the sense that their demands on the firm are inappropriate, they had better give "legitimacy" to these groups in terms of their ability to affect the direction of the firm. Hence, "legitimacy" can be understood in a managerial sense implying that it is "legitimate to spend time and resources" on stakeholders, regardless of the appropriateness of their demands.
>
> There is, of course, a broader notion of legitimacy which is at issue here. Do all stakeholders have an equally "legitimate" claim on the resources of the corporation? . . . For the present time I shall put these questions aside. . . (Freeman, 1984: 45)

This passage set a closely followed precedent among stakeholder scholars. Considerations of stakeholder legitimacy are deemed by nearly all to be important but in the determination of legitimacy, scholars and managers are left largely to their own devices. As in Freeman's original discussion, scholars of stakeholder theory note the importance of stakeholder legitimacy to the theory and move on. This creates some ambiguity within stakeholder theory.

This ambiguity regarding stakeholder legitimacy manifests itself in the "broad vs. narrow" debate. On some broad conceptions it has been suggested that groups such as activists, competitors, and the natural environment be considered stakeholders. These authors generally appeal to Freeman's definition, "those who can affect or are affected by the achievement of the firm's objectives," as well as the intuition that the theory should account for as many stakeholders as possible to be adequately generalizable and comprehensive. However, an overly broad definition threatens the meaningfulness of the term *stakeholder*. If everyone is a stakeholder of everyone else, little value is added by the theory.

Alternatively, narrow conceptions conclude that only those groups to whom a moral obligation is owed be considered stakeholders, thereby omitting strategically important constituencies from the theory (e.g., activists and competitors). Many of those scholars who explicitly argue for a normative foundation for stakeholder theory adopt a narrow conception.[199] They mostly suggest that moral legitimacy is the *sine qua non* of stakeholder status. In these cases, stakeholder status is equivalent to moral legitimacy and those groups without such legitimacy should not be considered stakeholders. A theory of strategic management, however, would appear significantly incomplete in failing to consider the potential impact of powerful constituencies that could help or hinder the achievement of the organization's strategic objectives.

Donaldson and Preston recognize this problem when they write:

> Excessive breadth in the identification of stakeholders has arisen from a tendency to adopt definitions such as "anything influencing or influenced by" the firm. . . . The two types of interests that have cropped up most frequently in this connection are (a) competitors and (b) the media. . . . It is essential to draw a clear distinction between influencers and stakeholders: some actors in the enterprise (e.g., large investors) may be both, but some recognizable stakeholders (e.g., the job applicants) have no influence, and some influencers (e.g., the media) have no stakes.[200]

Though plausible, the stakeholder/influencer distinction remains underdetermined, notwithstanding its centrality. The most plausible interpretation of the distinction would be a narrow construal suggesting that influencers such as competitors and the media are not stakeholders. That is, the purpose of the organization cannot be to advance the well-being of competitors and the media; therefore, competitors are not stakeholders. It could be asked, however, whether stakeholder theory so described includes such "influencers." Are they stakeholders or not stakeholders? If they are not stakeholders, can they be considered part of stakeholder theory? If stakeholder theory is to be a theory of *strategic management and ethics*, then competitors cannot lie outside the theory. Strategy is centrally concerned with competitors, and stakeholder theory is incomplete without a mechanism for such concern. The question then becomes how to account for competitors without lumping them together with, for example, employees. Unlike Donaldson and Preston, Mitchell, Agle, and Wood,[201] argue that powerful constituencies *are* stakeholders.

Mitchell, Agle, and Wood propose a "theory of stakeholder identification and salience" (TSIS) they claim to be "comprehensive and useful." It is worth noting that it is the tension between these two qualities (comprehensiveness and usefulness) that provides much of the fodder for the "broad vs. narrow" debate. Their solution to the debate is summarized as follows:

> As a bridging concept, we argue that the broad concept of stakeholder management must be better defined in order to serve the narrower interests of legitimate stakeholders. Otherwise, influencing groups with power over the firm can disrupt operations so severely that *legitimate* claims cannot be met and the firm may not survive. *Yet, at the same time, it is important to recognize the legitimacy of some claims over others.*[202]

One cause of this confusion is that, within stakeholder research, legitimacy has generally been synonymous with *moral* legitimacy. It is problematic, however, to refer to powerful groups, to whom no moral obligation is owed but can nevertheless significantly affect the organization, as illegitimate or nonlegitimate.[203] Such reference runs contrary to much existing stakeholder scholarship, the extensive literature on legitimacy in other fields such as legal, political, and moral theory, and organization studies—presumably among the fields upon which stakeholder researchers would hope to draw and to which they would aspire to contribute. Stakeholder theory must somehow resolve these inconsistencies.

In the following section a distinction is defended between normative and derivative stakeholder legitimacy. This distinction provides a middle ground in the broad versus narrow debate that recognizes the moral obligations of the organization to some (narrow) group of stakeholders while at the same time accounting for the pragmatic, power-based conception of legitimacy prominent in organization theory and sociology as well as broader approaches to stakeholder theory.[204] In short, the distinction between normative and derivative legitimacy brings together both moral philosophical and strategic conceptions of stakeholder theory and thereby integrates these two often opposing streams of stakeholder research.

Legitimacy in Stakeholder Research: Normative and Derivative Perspectives

Stakeholder theory can be rendered more precise and consistent—both internally and with other overlapping literatures—if the central idea of legitimacy is understood in terms of normative legitimacy and derivative legitimacy.[a] These two conceptions reflect the intuition in stakeholder theorizing that some stakeholders merit greater moral consideration in managerial decision making than

---

[a]The use of the terms *normative* and *derivative* is intended as an implicit reference to Donaldson & Preston's categories of stakeholder research. I am aware that Donaldson & Preston were describing varieties of stakeholder *research* rather than stakeholder *groups* themselves. Despite this potential for confusion, these terms are more descriptive of the relevant stakeholder relationships than such alternative terms as "primary and secondary," "internal and external," or "voluntary and involuntary" stakeholders. For example, customers are "external" to the organization while employees are "internal," but both are considered, on most accounts, to be groups to whom a moral obligation is due and hence "normative" stakeholders.

others, but that the theory would be incomplete if it failed to account for stakeholders who might have a significant effect upon the organization and the achievement of its goals. For many prominent theorists, however, not only is stakeholder legitimacy a normative concept, but the normative features of the framework are foundational to the other (i.e., descriptive and instrumental) aspects.

Donaldson and Preston argue that normative aspects of the theory serve as the foundation for the theory in all its forms. They illustrate this by showing how descriptive and instrumental stakeholder research fails to justify reliance on a stakeholder theory of management. They argue that the empirical evidence is inadequate, and the analytical arguments ultimately rely on more than an instrumental rationale; it is the normative core that justifies stakeholder theory. Freeman elaborates on the importance to stakeholder theory of including reference to some "normative core" and Jones and Wicks argue that "any instrumental theory with its roots in the stakeholder concept must have morally acceptable ends and means . . ."[205]

Normative Legitimacy   Normative stakeholders, then, are those stakeholders to whom the organization has a moral obligation, an obligation of stakeholder fairness, over and above that due other social actors simply by virtue of their being human.[206] These groups are the answer to the seminal stakeholder question, For whose benefit . . . should the firm be managed? When it is indicated that a particular group is owed no *stakeholder-based* obligations, it would be a mistake to interpret this as meaning that the organization has no moral relationship whatsoever with that group. Simply because a person or group does not merit the additional moral consideration conferred upon normative stakeholders does not mean that they may be morally disregarded. One still may not break promises without sufficient cause, kill competitors for market share, or violate the rights of or otherwise act immorally toward these groups[b]. However, no *additional* moral consideration is due these groups in managerial decision making and the organization has no special obligation to attend to their well-being.

The violation of human rights by an organization would fall under this proviso. The use of forced labor, racial/ethnic/sexual discrimination, lying and breaking contracts, and egregious pollution of the natural environment are likely examples of activities that would be wrong irrespective of the stakeholder status of the victims. These violations may occur against a group or individual who is also a normative stakeholder, but it is not due only, or even primarily, to this stakeholder status that these actions are morally prohibited. They are wrong for reasons prior to any stakeholder obligation that may obtain.

Perhaps Max Clarkson put it best when he wrote, "Stakeholder theory should not be used to weave a basket big enough to hold the world's misery."[207] Stakeholder theory is not intended as—and is indeed ill suited to the needs of—a comprehensive moral scheme. It is instead limited to positive obligations arising in an organizational context. To deny that a group is a normative stakeholder is not to take anything away from that group to which it was previously entitled, rather it denies the existence of an additional obligation of stakeholder fairness.

Derivative Legitimacy Derivatively legitimate stakeholders are those groups whose actions and claims must be accounted for by managers due to their potential effects upon the normative stakeholders. Managerial attention to these groups is legitimate; but this legitimacy is derived from their ability to affect the organization and its normative stakeholders, consideration

---

[b]Donaldson & Dunfee's (1999) notion of hypernorms captures well the idea that there is a set of moral minimums that apply to all humans regardless of any particular social relationships in which they may find themselves. See also Rawls (1993) on the idea of an overlapping consensus.

FIGURE 1   Traditional Stakeholder Map

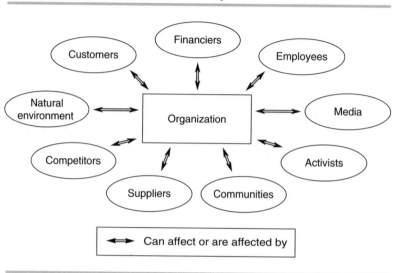

of these groups is justifiably limited to this ability to affect the organization and its normative stakeholders. The legitimacy of the derivative stakeholders is based solely on obligations owed to others and does not result from any obligation due the derivative stakeholders themselves. Figures 1, 2, and 3 graphically demonstrate the normative/derivative distinction as well as the difference between previous stakeholder thinking and that described here. The relationships depicted are merely for illustrative purposes and do not reflect any specific organization's stakeholder map. Still less is it a representation of all organizations and their stakeholder relationships.

Returning to the example suggested by Donaldson and Preston, to the extent that the news media can help or hinder organizational objectives, managers should be aware of these effects. Managers need not necessarily concern themselves with the well-being of the news media as they would their share owners. But, to the extent that the media can affect share owners' well-being and share owners are normative stakeholders, managers should take account of these effects and manage

FIGURE 2 Activists as Derivative Stakeholders

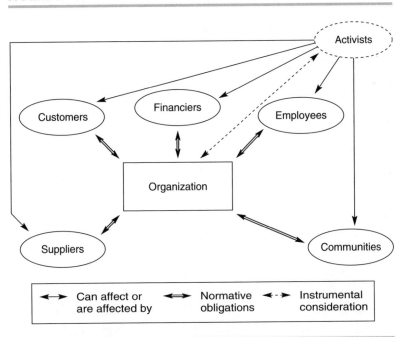

FIGURE 3 Stakeholder Map—Legitimate, Derivative, and Non-Stakeholders

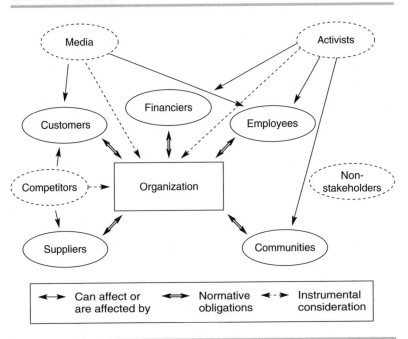

them in the best interest of the share owners, the organization, and its normative stakeholders.

A group may be considered a derivative stakeholder in either a salutary or derogatory sense. A group may be derivative in that it represents or may advance the interests of the organization and its normative stakeholders. Favorable media coverage is an example of this sort of instrumentality. The organization may wish to assist in this coverage, but still has no obligation by virtue of this coverage to attend to the well-being of the media organization. Derivative status may also result when a group wishes to do harm to the organization or its normative stakeholders. Competitors are a good example of this type of stakeholder, as would be a terrorist group who wishes nothing but to cause the cessation of operations by the focal firm.

The description of derivative stakeholders bears some resemblance to what Mitchell et al. call "dangerous" or "dormant" stakeholders. Dangerous or dormant stakeholders can affect the corporation but have no legitimate relationship with the organization (according to their understanding of legitimacy). How is the taxonomy proposed here different from the theory of stakeholder identification and salience (TSIS)? Isn't derivative legitimacy just another name for power? There are several reasons why conceiving of coercive power as derivative legitimacy may add value to stakeholder theory.

To begin, the conception of derivative legitimacy encompasses the notion of power, but is more comprehensive and more consistent with the myriad notions of legitimacy in the organization studies literature as well as previous stakeholder writings. Power has frequently been conceived of as a basis for legitimacy in and of itself,[208] and the normative/derivative distinction recognizes this while still maintaining the important moral distinctions among the different derivations of legitimacy. Conceiving of power as a distinct attribute from legitimacy runs counter to the received literature on legitimacy in both organization studies as well as stakeholder theory.

Also, the idea of derivative legitimacy emphasizes why powerful stakeholders are important and makes explicit the normative (moral) reasons for attending to groups that wield power with no moral legitimacy. It is not merely for the sake of self-interest that managers must attend to the demands of powerful stakeholders; rather, it is due to the obligations to all normative stakeholders. The *moral* reasons for attending to the demands of powerful stakeholders are made explicit and the centrality of the normative foundations of stakeholder theory are emphasized. Hence, this conception of legitimacy is consistent with the "pragmatic experimentation" approach: "organization studies as a vehicle to help people lead better lives."[209]

Finally, reference to derivatively legitimate stakeholders rather than powerful stakeholders avoids problems associated with stakeholder latency. Mitchell et al. "suggest that a theory of stakeholder identification and salience must somehow account for *latent* stakeholders if it is to be both comprehensive and useful, because such identification can, at a minimum, help organizations avoid problems and perhaps even enhance effectiveness."[210] On this typology, a group can be a stakeholder "without being in actual relationship with the firm." However, among the compelling arguments in favor of a narrow interpretation of stakeholder theory are managerial time constraints and limited cognitive capacity. A stakeholder theory that requires a manager to consider those with whom the organization has no relationship whatsoever bends too far toward comprehensiveness to the detriment of usefulness.

The Mitchell et al. theory of stakeholder identification and salience is able to counter that such "dormant" stakeholders will actually achieve low managerial salience and hence there will be little loss of practical usefulness. It is noteworthy, however, that the scholarly antecedents upon which Mitchell et al. rely, as well as their own analysis of power, explicitly refer to the existence of "a social relationship"[211] providing evidence of ambiguity or ambivalence even within TSIS.

The importance of most "dormant" stakeholders to managerial decision making is so small that one might reasonably question the need for their inclusion in the framework at all. The inclusion of all groups that may be *potentially* affected by a managerial decision drives the framework straight back into the abyss of stakeholder proliferation and intractability from which the "theory of stakeholder identification and salience" was intended to save it. If mere coercive power is considered insufficient as a qualification for normative stakeholder status and instead a relationship of derivative legitimacy is required (i.e., a relationship in which there is some reason to believe the powerful entity intends to exercise this power over the organization and its normative stakeholders), then the issues surrounding latent stakeholders become less problematic and stakeholder theory rendered more practicable.

Using the term *derivative stakeholder* also has advantages over Donaldson and Preston's "influencers." Reference to derivative stakeholders leaves no ambiguity regarding the applicability of the theory to these groups. They are stakeholders and therefore part of stakeholder theory. Further, the term is descriptive of these groups' relationship to the organization and its other stakeholders. They are legitimate objects of managerial attention, but the legitimacy is derivative and not direct.

Non-stakeholders   Certain groups and individuals are not stakeholders at all. The focal organization has no moral obligation to these groups and individuals in addition to what is their due *as humans* (i.e., no stakeholder-based obligation), and the likelihood of their having an impact upon the organization or its other normative stakeholders is minimal. As such, managers may justifiably omit these groups and individuals from the decision-making process.

This last category—non-stakeholder—has been historically underemphasized in the literature. The size and definition of this category contains the core of the broad versus narrow debate that has so occupied stakeholder scholars, and is central to the managerial usability of the framework. If the concept of legitimacy described here is correct, power and legitimacy cannot be severed as suggested by TSIS and its adherents. There is only legitimacy—power is but one avenue by which it is acquired.

One implication of this is that the term *stakeholder* may well imply "legitimacy" and *illegitimate stakeholder* may be a contradiction. Thus, if it is legitimate to attend to the demands or well-being of a group, that group is a stakeholder. It is still important to be aware of the source of the legitimacy inasmuch as normative stakeholders bear different treatment and managerial consideration than derivative stakeholders.

Legitimacy in Practice

Several points bear mention regarding this taxonomy. Note that it will be difficult to draw clear lines between the various categories. Stakeholder status can change across both time and issue. Given the right circumstances, non-stakeholders can become derivative or normative stakeholders; the normative bond between a stakeholder group and an organization may be severed so that former normative stakeholders become non-stakeholders; or an individual might cease being a member of a stakeholder group and thereby cease being a stakeholder (at least in that capacity). Such changes in stakeholder status will also be a function of the normative justification relied upon, but openness to such dynamism will be a feature of any defensible normative core.

It is also important to note that within the stakeholder categories, the level of managerial attention and obligation will admit of degrees. Not all normative stakeholders will necessarily be due *equal* consideration. Rather, *equity* would better characterize the relationship such that each receives consideration based on contribution to the organization (see Chapter 2). For example, a large shareholder would justifiably receive greater voice in decision making and a greater share of the organizational rewards than would a small supplier or remote community member.

Also, in some instances managers may spend the majority of their time attending to the demands of derivative stakeholders. This is consistent with the framework sketched here. The priority of normative legitimacy to derivative legitimacy is a logical and moral one and not necessarily indicative of which groups will receive managerial attention and in what degree. This framework helps to prioritize stakeholders by indicating which groups have a greater claim to voice in decision making and to the outcomes of organizational activities.

The normative defense of a broad stakeholder theory relies on the distinction between the two types of legitimacy described earlier. This conception of stakeholder legitimacy is able to reference a normative core and a moral conception of legitimacy, while not discounting the important strategic features of derivative legitimacy. Appeal to a distinction between normative and derivative stakeholders retains the conceptual rigor of the narrow conception and its reference to a moral foundation, while also exhibiting the breadth required of a comprehensive theory of managerial decision making.

Consistent with previous stakeholder literature, as well as research in organization studies, stakeholder legitimacy is sensitive to the dynamic nature of stakeholder relations. It may be the case that the activist group is not so radical as was first believed and that they in fact represent the views of a large percentage of the organization's employees, customers, and communities. In this case, the map may look much the same, but managerial action should be different. Management should attend to the protesters in a more constructive way as proxies for the interests of normative stakeholders. The protesters themselves are still derivative stakeholders, but management should now take a more cooperative and less antagonistic approach than in the earlier situation. The extent to which the activists' demands are consistent with the views of some normative stakeholder may also change.

The actual impact of the protests and which groups of normative stakeholders are affected will also vary across time. If the relationship between the group and the organization moves from antagonism to close cooperation, the activist group may even rise to the status of normative stakeholder (e.g., some environmental groups have started working closely with petroleum companies on sensitive projects). These differences are matters for empirical investigation by managers and researchers and are also dependent upon the normative foundation used.

Finally, different issues will imply different points of emphasis on the stakeholder map and different involved stakeholder groups. Favorable or unfavorable press will require attention to the media as derivative stakeholders. Competitors are nearly ubiquitous in the ability to affect the organization and would hence qualify as derivative stakeholders for myriad issues. For other issues the focus may be on one or more normative stakeholders. Employees would be central to the issue of a change in the pension plan, customers to a problem with product quality, and shareholders to a prospective change in the dividend.

The distinction between normative, derivative, and non-stakeholders is vital to both scholars and managers. Managers have distinct ethical obligations to normative stakeholders that may not exist with regard to derivative or non-stakeholders and these obligations will dictate a different sort of managerial attention and treatment. Broadly, normative stakeholders are the answer to the question, For whose benefit . . . should the firm be managed? While stakeholder theory would be managerially incomplete without consideration of competitors, surely the firm is not to be managed for the benefit of the competition. Though both are legitimate stakeholders, it seems clear that employees should get a voice in determining the direction of the organization in a way that competitors should not. Similarly, managers are justified in ignoring or attempting to undermine certain powerless, nonlegitimate groups, but may not justifiably ignore or attempt to undermine share owners; and this is not simply due to the asymmetries of power, but to the moral legitimacy of the latter and the absence of the same by the former.

Though it cannot be entirely determinate in the abstract, the distinction also helps managers and scholars with prioritizing stakeholder demands. It is for the benefit of the normatively legitimate stakeholders that the organization is managed and their concerns are primary. Attention to derivative stakeholder demands is derivative and hence logically secondary, though these demands may still occupy greater managerial attention at any given time.

In addition to improving the justification and specification of stakeholder management, improved clarity, consistency, and precision regarding the concept of legitimacy will also help future stakeholder research and theorizing. Descriptive research on how managers actually make decisions involving stakeholders and stakeholder salience may bear greater (or lesser) similarity between stakeholder prescriptions and managerial actions than has hitherto been found. The prescriptions regarding prioritization of constituencies and derivative legitimacy could be tested to ascertain whether this framework improves stakeholder and public perceptions of organizational morality as well as more traditional measures of organization success (e.g., profitability). Future normative stakeholder theorizing will need to attend to the legitimacy of attention to derivative stakeholders. The most direct effect on stakeholder theorizing will be the recognition of the multidimensional character of legitimacy. Though normatively based, legitimacy is not exclusively a normative construct. This recognition will bring stakeholder theorizing into greater consistency with its fellow disciplines such as organization studies, sociology, and philosophy.

CHAPTER 7

Stakeholder Identity

The meaning of this term is so porous that there is little
interpretation it seems able to resist. . . .

—ISAIAH BERLIN[212]

L ack of clarity on the issue of stakeholder legitimacy has
created ambiguity on the question of stakeholder identity.[213] That is, who are the organization's stakeholders? In
Chapter 5 I argued that obligations of stakeholder fairness create direct moral (normative) obligations. Stakeholders are
those groups from whom the organization has voluntarily
accepted benefits and to whom there arises a moral obligation.
In Chapter 6 I argued that stakeholder status may also be
derived from the power to affect the organization and its normative stakeholders. This provides one answer to the problem
of stakeholder identity. This chapter will examine how the preceding arguments resolve the stakeholder status of specific,
long-contested candidates for stakeholder identity: the natural
environment and activists.

The Natural Environment as a Stakeholder

An example of theoretical uncertainty caused by the problem of stakeholder legitimacy is the status of the natural environment within a stakeholder framework. Is the natural environment a stakeholder? Mark Starik has argued for the affirmative.[214] On a fairness-based approach, it is less clear that such a case can be made. In this and the next two sections I will describe Starik's work on the stakeholder status of the natural environment, argue for why the natural environment is not and cannot be a normative stakeholder, and demonstrate how the natural environment may, nonetheless, be accounted for from within a fairness-based stakeholder approach.

Starik has written that the non-human natural environment merits stakeholder status. He goes on to suggest and argue against three reasons for the historical omission of the natural environment as "one or more stakeholders." His arguments are suggestive of why the problem of stakeholder identity is, in fact, a problem for stakeholder theory more generally. Hence, it will prove helpful to analyze his arguments in favor of stakeholder status for non-human nature.

Starik arranges his essay around three answers to the question, "Why hasn't non-human nature been considered a stakeholder?" His first answer is the rather obvious and tightly circular, "'Stakeholder' status has been restricted to humans only." The section heading notwithstanding, Starik's goal is to give a brief discussion of a number of definitions of the term *stakeholder* and point out the fact that, with two exceptions, the natural environment has been excluded from the definition.

In response to this shortcoming, Starik suggests that the natural environment is in fact a business environment. Quoting Donna Wood,[215] Starik writes:

> She identified the "stakeholder principle" as "(a) company's stakeholders are affected by its actions, and stakeholders can affect the way a company does business. Managers, therefore, are

obliged to understand the stakeholders in the firm's *environment* and their relationships to the firm."[216]

Starik here plays on the dual meanings of the term *environment*. Whereas Wood is discussing environment in the sense of the social context and situations within which business operates, Starik means this type of environment as well as the natural, non-human ecological environment; thus, he emphasizes environment to show that the natural environment is inclusive of both meanings of the term.

Starik is, correct in his connection of the natural environment with the business environment. Nature provides a great many of the constraints on not only business life, but also on all aspects of human existence. The question we must ask, and indeed the problem of stakeholder identity itself, is, What is the necessary connection between something's existence as a constraint on business and that thing's status as a stakeholder?

One answer is to appeal to the standard definitions of stakeholder in the literature as Starik does. The natural environment affects the organization; affecting the organization is, on some definitions, a sufficient condition for stakeholder status; therefore, the natural environment, and everything in it, is one or more stakeholders. However, this only serves to push the question back a level: What is it about an entity's ability to affect the organization that qualifies it as meriting stakeholder status? Further, if anything that affects or can affect the corporation qualifies as a stakeholder, then what is excluded from this definition?

Starik's second answer is " [the] 'stakeholder' idea has been an exclusively political-economic concept." That is, non-humans do not and cannot wield the necessary political and economic power to have their "voices" heard by the organization.

In response, Starik suggests that in fact the natural environment does possess economic value and political "voice" that "can be heard continuously throughout the natural environment for all humans to heed or appreciate. . . ."[217]

Furthermore, even if nature does not have the appropriate political "voice," it may nonetheless qualify as a stakeholder on the "affect or affected by" criteria. He suggests a similarity between the natural environment and historically disenfranchised groups such as "slaves, indigenous peoples, women, minorities, the homeless, abused children, and political prisoners" who, although having no political voice, would nevertheless qualify as stakeholders on his account.

The majority of Starik's argument regarding the political-economic essence of non-human nature deals with how non-human nature goes *beyond* being solely a political-economic entity. That is, certain ethical and legal facets of non-human entities, Starik implies, strengthen their case for stakeholder status. He invokes the language of "obligations" to make his arguments.

> One well-known stakeholder proponent (Carroll, 1989, 1993a), for instance, has developed the moral legitimacy aspect of stakeholder management, in which those human individuals and organizations to whom an organization is morally obligated are included as stakeholders. If this *ethical* aspect of stakeholder management is credible, the development of environmental ethics implies that the natural environment also can be considered as one or more stakeholders of organizations. The environmental ethic of wise stewardship of natural resources, for instance, implies that organizations are morally obligated to respect non-human nature's bounty and limits (Leopold, 1949), and, therefore, its role as a potential stakeholder of these organizations.[218]

On Starik's view, then, the ethical nature of stakeholder theory combined with the appropriate environmental ethic bolsters the case for the environment as one or more stakeholders.

The final answer to the question of why non-human nature has not been considered a stakeholder is that it already has human beings acting as proxies on its behalf, thus rendering unnecessary stakeholder status for non-humans. The existence of the Environmental Protection Agency, Department of the

Interior, National Resources Defense Council, and Sierra Club renders stakeholder status for the natural environment redundant or unnecessary.

Starik suggests, however, "Human environmental stakeholders are necessary but not sufficient."

> [A]n industrial worker's employment interests can be represented by herself, her union, her supervisor, her top manager and her jurisdiction's government agencies.[219]

Thus, we see the feasibility of having one stakeholder represented by a multitude of groups; given the decline in quality of many natural environments, the current number of groups representing the non-human nature is "apparently not sufficient to protect non-human nature's 'stakes'" on Starik's view. Furthermore, the contentiousness among the groups that are ostensibly proxies for the natural environment diminishes the effectiveness of the human proxies. Hence, the following occurs.

> [T]he continued human-caused environmental deterioration of the planet appears to call for all organizations to consider as stakeholders as many natural environment entities as possible.[220]

These then represent Starik's arguments in favor of stakeholder status for the natural environment. In the next section I analyze Starik's arguments, both on their own merits and from within a fairness-based approach to stakeholder management.

Problems with the Natural Environment as a Stakeholder

Recall Starik's quotation from Wood: "Managers, therefore, are obliged to understand the stakeholders in the firm's *environment* and their relationships to the firm." The important thing is that even in this passage, the business environment and stakeholders are distinct constructs. Wood distinguishes the business environment from stakeholders *in the firm's environment.* Even granting Starik's assertion that the natural environment is an important part of a firm's business environment, this does not lead to the conclusion that the natural environment is one or more stakeholders. Surely the presence of an entity within a firm's business environment cannot create moral obligations in addition to those duties that exist prior to business interaction. If this is the case, then everything that exists within the organizational environment also merits stakeholder status.

What of Starik's claim that things in the business environment and hence things in the natural environment can affect the organization and, therefore, the natural environment is definitive of stakeholder status? This is precisely the problem of stakeholder identity. An entity's ability to affect the organization is, at best, an inadequately discriminating criterion for establishing moral obligations—as stakeholder theory must surely do. There can be no additional moral consideration demanded nor obligation created merely based on one entity's ability to affect another. Your ability to run over my dog, thus grieving me deeply, could hardly mean that I have a moral obligation to consider the effects on you of my future actions above and beyond the duties I owe you as a person. If all stakeholder status means is that I have duties to consider the effects of my actions on all humans, then what does calling someone a stakeholder add to one's status as a human?

In the preceding paragraph, however, the talk is of duties that are owed to others *qua* human being. This is precisely the point of the second prong of Starik's argument: The assumption that the non-human natural environment is not a political-economic entity suggests not only that it is not a stakeholder, but also that it *cannot* be a stakeholder. It is precisely the language of the previous description of *human* duties that precludes consideration of the natural environment as a stakeholder or any moral consideration at all.

Does, however, excluding an entity from stakeholder status imply that the entity is therefore excluded from all moral consideration? Surely not; yet Starik takes this approach. For example, he writes:

> However, even if many *current* organizations do not pay credence to the fact that non-human nature has a "voice," that may be still not be [sic] a sound reason to exclude nature from consideration as one or more stakeholders of organizations.[221]

It is not beholden upon the theorist or manager to come up with reasons to "exclude or not exclude" a particular group from stakeholder status. Rather, it is the job of the theorist to suggest reasons for *inclusion* of an entity as a stakeholder group. We may grant Starik the suggestion that the non-human natural environment merits moral consideration without the further conclusion that, the natural environment is one or more stakeholders.

In this same context, Starik goes on to suggest that the natural environment is an entity "*beyond a solely political-economic one.* Since its popularization in the literature in 1984, the stakeholder concept has developed ethical, socio-emotional, legal, and physical connotations as well."[222] The argument seems to be that since stakeholder theory has these facets in addition to political-economic aspects, and the natural environment also has similar characteristics, then the environment must be a stakeholder. Similarly, then, one might argue that a manager's relationship with her spouse has moral implications and her relationships with her subordinates are of moral importance. Both types of relationships have ethical, socioemotional, and legal aspects. Therefore, her subordinates are all her spouses or that her spouse is her subordinate. This does not follow.

It is, again, quite possible that both stakeholder theory and organizational relationships with the natural environment have all of the connotations attributed by Starik. It does not follow, however, that one is therefore a subset of the other.

Starik leans heavily in this section once again on the "can affect" part of Freeman's definition of a stakeholder. The inadequacy of this criterion has already been discussed.

Finally, what of Starik's claim that human proxies for the natural environment are necessary, but not sufficient? Part of the problem with the sufficiency of human stakeholder proxies, on Starik's account, is that these groups often spend a lot of time arguing among themselves, thus "leading to less than ecologically-supporting compromises." This hardly looks like an argument for more of such groups. Indeed, if the groups that currently exist "experience significant internal strife and resource limitations," then would not having more of them *increase* the contentiousness and further stretch the already thin budgets of the extant groups?

The argument in this section, and indeed much of Starik's essay, can be summarized in the following passage:

> [T]he continued human-caused environmental deterioration of the planet appears to call for all organizations to consider as stakeholders as many natural environment entities as possible.[223]

Thus, it is the deterioration of the planet that ultimately justifies stakeholder status for the natural environment. Additionally, the natural environment represents as many stakeholders as possible and these entities are to be stakeholders of all organizations. This is the problem of stakeholder identity run amok. People cannot be deemed stakeholders simply because they have problems. Stakeholder theory is not intended as comprehensive moral theory. It merely describes the obligations that result from a special organizational relationship. Those outside these special relations should look elsewhere for relief.

Does stakeholder theory, then, have nothing to say concerning the degradation of the natural environment? This is where the third part of Starik's argument becomes interesting, because if stakeholder theory is to be useful in lessening the organizational and economic burdens on the natural environment, it *must* be through the obligations between organizations and their human stakeholders.

The Natural Environment and Community Stakeholders

A point of controversy in environmental ethics, the term *anthropocentric* indicates that the theory deals exclusively in terms of human beings and is concerned only with the rights, duties, obligations, actions, and so forth of human beings. It is contrasted with, for example, an eco-centric theory that would take the unit of analysis to be ecosystems and would likely include arguments concerning the rights of, duties to, or moral considerability of non-human natural entities. An anthropocentric theory of environmental ethics would likely argue that the environment ought to be better shepherded because of the danger of environmental damage to currently extant humans and/or unborn future generations of persons.[224] A non-anthropocentric (eco-centric) theory, on the other hand, would likely argue that the natural environment ought not be damaged, not due to the effects of such damage on the relevant human population, but because the non-human natural environment and its component parts themselves merit some sort of rights or other moral considerability.[225]

It is probably clear from the preceding that, on a fairness-based theory of stakeholders, only humans can be stakeholders of an organization, because only humans are capable of generating the necessary obligations for stakeholder status. Only humans are capable of the necessary volitionality in the acceptance of benefits of a mutually beneficial cooperative scheme. Stakeholder theory is anthropocentric.

The anthropocentric nature of stakeholder theory does not, however, imply that managers need not consider the environment at all. Just as an anthropocentric environmental ethic is nonetheless an environmental ethic, so too can environmental considerations arise for managers within a stakeholder framework. There are at least two reasons why managers must morally consider the environment in decision making despite the natural environment not qualifying as a stakeholder.

1. The natural environment may retain moral considerability regardless of stakeholder status.
2. The obligations owed to other stakeholders will likely dictate managerial diligence regarding the natural environment.

First, stakeholder theory does not claim to be a comprehensive moral theory. There are myriad moral considerations that simply do not fall within the purview of stakeholder obligations. Just as promise-keeping, though a moral precept, is not exhaustive of morality, so too is stakeholder theory not exhaustive of ethics even within organizational contexts. Though a powerful framework for deriving and interpreting many ethical issues in organizations, stakeholder theory nevertheless exists within a backdrop of social and moral rules and mores that also dictate behavior both within and outside the organizational and managerial context. Included among the actions that do not receive a great deal of attention within stakeholder theory (or indeed within any obligation, duties, or rights-based moral theory) are considerations of supererogation. One could take an infinite number of actions that, although not morally requisite, would certainly qualify as morally praiseworthy. Hence, even without stakeholder status, certain actions are morally prohibited (such as murder or theft) and other actions are morally praiseworthy, regardless of stakeholder status of the potential object of the action.

Kenneth Goodpaster makes persuasive arguments for the "moral considerability" of non-humans.[226] He argues: "Nothing short of the condition of *being alive* seems to me to be a plausible and nonarbitrary criterion."[227] He finds sentience and the capacity for interests as arbitrary conditions for moral considerability. What is interesting about Goodpaster's approach is that he does not argue for the *rights* of non-humans nor even that non-humans merit the same degree of moral considerability as humans. Instead he argues that non-humans merit some sort of consideration in moral decision making by virtue of being alive.

Goodpaster's as well as any number of other arguments (anthropocentric and nonanthropocentric alike) for a moral imperative of environmental stewardship are all suggestive of non-stakeholder-based reasons for conserving the earth's natural resources and preserving bio-diversity. Stakeholder explanations are, therefore, unnecessary for the conclusion that managers ought to consider non-human natural environment entities in their decision making.

Although unnecessary, however, there are reasons involving the obligations due legitimate stakeholders for considering the natural environment in managerial decision making. This brings us to the second manner in which the natural environment is likely to receive consideration in managerial decision making within a stakeholder framework.

The communities within which organizations operate are universally counted among the stakeholders of such organizations. That organizations are cooperatively engaged with their communities for mutual gain is obvious. Further, organizations benefit voluntarily from this cooperative interaction with their communities. As such, according to the principle of stakeholder fairness, the organization and its managers have an obligation to consider the well-being of the communities within which they operate.

A substantial portion of a community's well-being is the health and integrity of that community's natural environment. The direction of the argument is likely to be clear at this point. The organization has an obligation, not to the non-human natural environment itself, but to the community within which it operates, to be a good steward of at least local environmental resources.[a]

This sort of derivative relationship is generalizable to a number of historically problematic stakeholder groups. Despite the absence of obligations of stakeholder fairness, and hence normative legitimacy, between the organization and some constituencies there remain convincing reasons for conceiving of them as stakeholders: derivatively legitimate stakeholders. Another constituency that has proven historically awkward for stakeholder theory is the social activist group. The next section takes up the stakeholder status of such groups.

Social Activists as Stakeholders

The arguments regarding the stakeholder status of social activists look much the same as the arguments regarding the natural environment. Though I will not undertake a discussion of the same depth as that just presented, the arguments will be largely recognizable from the preceding discussion.

Activists have undoubtedly incited a great deal of change in a number of industries. One such example is the impact AIDS activists have had on the pharmaceutical industry. Many such activists have employed what others consider illegitimate actions to draw attention to themselves and their cause.[228] The methods for drawing this attention are well publicized and include interrupting the filming of the television show *Midnight Caller*, invading the New York Stock Exchange (waving signs saying sell Burroughs-Wellcome), shutting down the Golden Gate bridge, harassing a former NYC health commissioner (including throwing paint at his house, occupying his office, and generally harassing him and his family both at

---

[a]This argument assumes that the community in question considers part of its well-being to be the health of its surrounding environment. Indeed, inasmuch as environmental issues are most often matters of degree, it should be a cooperative effort between the community and the organization to determine the appropriate level of environmental concern. Such a discursive method of deriving stakeholder norms is discussed in Chapter 5.

home and at restaurants), storming St. Patrick's Cathedral during mass throwing condoms and desecrating the Host, and numerous other protests of varying types. At the Sixth International Conference on AIDS in San Francisco, ACT-UP was—for them—well behaved as they ignored a call for "a f___ing riot" by founder Larry Kramer. Instead, conference organizers went to great pains to include HIV patients in the planning and, as described in *The Fragile Coalition* by Dr. Robert Wachter, the program's director, what could have meant the end of this important meeting of scientists instead brought AIDS activists closer to the mainstream and established a greater environment of communication.

Interest groups are nothing new in the United States. James Madison wrote of faction in Federalist No. 10.[229] Madison saw the inevitable rise of faction as a necessary evil in a properly functioning republic and argued that rather than trying to control the causes of faction, the effects should be tempered.

Interest groups are generally the purview of political scientists and as such the majority of treatises on the topic concern themselves with interest group activities vis-à-vis the government(s). This position is proper because, historically, the focus of interest group activity has been government. A recent development is that in keeping with the growing disenchantment of the citizenry with the governmental process and politicians, interest groups are increasingly circumventing the government and going straight to the source of their angst—business organizations. AIDS activists are taking their case directly to the pharmaceutical companies in a manner similar to that of environmentalists Earth First!, antiabortionists Operation Rescue, and animal rights activists PETA, among others. Of course, much of the impact of activists still comes through the vehicle of government agencies, but the successful use of boycotts, proxy battles, and direct public action against companies *and their executives* indicates continued and likely increasing use of such extragovernmental approaches—a trend that must assuredly interest every executive in the world.

The question for current purposes regards the moral status of such activist groups vis-à-vis the corporation. Do these activist groups merit the additional moral consideration due normative stakeholders? The answer depends largely on the particular relationship between the relevant activist group and the organization. Many of the highest profile activist groups are not cooperatively engaged with the organization. In fact, many such groups are overtly hostile and confrontational with the organization. As such, managers of an organization need not consider antagonistic social activists in the same moral light due normative stakeholders.

However, other activist groups engage cooperatively with other (typically business) organizations. Some environmental groups prefer cooperation to terrorism. Indeed, among the multiple groups that may represent a given cause, may be both cooperative and confrontational wings.[b] To the extent that the cooperative groups aid in the achievement of the goals of the cooperative scheme, they may be considered normative stakeholders on a fairness-based account with the concomitant moral obligations obtaining.

Assuming, however, that the activist group does not participate in the operations of the organization, they do not merit the status of normative stakeholder group. However, they may, nonetheless, merit managerial attention as derivative stakeholders. This may be the case in at least two different ways. They may merit managerial attention if they represent the actual views of other normative groups. For example, if an environmental activist group complains that a particular production facility is polluting the air and water of a given area and the employees or local communities (the former being a likely subset of the latter) have a similar complaint, then the organization and its managers must consider the demands of

---

[b]Consider as analogies Rev. Dr. Martin Luther King, Jr. & Malcolm X or the E.L.F. and the Sierra Club.

the activist group as a proxy for the desires of these norma-tively legitimate stakeholders. In this case the activist group does not merit consideration as a legitimate stakeholder, but they do merit attention nonetheless given the coincidence of their views with one or more normative stakeholder groups.

In cases when activists do, in fact, represent the sentiments of other normative stakeholder groups or society at large, the activists may be usefully considered as engaged in an activity that is similar to civil disobedience.[230] This idea merits a brief examination.

Activist Groups and Civil Disobedience

Civil disobedience[231] is usually thought to be directed at the civil government. From Plato's "*Crito*"[232] to Thoreau's "Civil Disobedience"[233] to the protests against the Vietnam conflict, government policy has historically been the object of the protest. At first glance, this seems quite appropriate. It is, after all, the laws of the civil government that are being disobeyed and the agents of the government who arrest, detain, and try the offenders. Often it *is* the policies of the government that are the objects of the disobedience as in these familiar exam-ples. Overlooked, however, are the equally famous and appar-ently increasing examples of civil disobedience aimed at com-mercial institutions. The issue has not gone completely unnoticed by academics. Michael Walzer's essay entitled, "Civil Disobedience and Corporate Authority,"[234] had a similar theme. Ray Jones has also elaborated on civil disobedience as a concept useful to scholars studying the interface between business and society.[235] However, these essays deal more with the case of internal constituents and disobedience (e.g., employee strikes), whereas here I am interested in extending the concept of civil disobedience to external constituencies.

In the common conception of civil disobedience, the disobe-diants appeal to society or, more commonly, its representative (i.e., the government) asserting that some generally held moral principle is not being properly observed. However, on some occasions it is not the government or its policies that are the proximal objects of the protest; rather, it is frequently the modern corporation that is being appealed to and the concept of civil disobedience can be useful in analyzing such a protest. All appeals are, in the end, to the majority in these cases. A more precise rendering of this thesis, then, is that while all civil disobedience is directed toward "society," the structure or institution of mediation between individuals or groups and society is most often government. Sometimes (increasingly more often), however, the modern corporation is the institution of mediation.

Indeed, the most famous practitioner of civil disobedience in American history was Rev. Dr. Martin Luther King, Jr. His "Letter from Birmingham City Jail" is a seminal work in the area of civil disobedience. While it is true that much of the work of the civil rights movement was directed at changing the laws and thus at the government at various levels, the true object at least some of the time was the economic equality to both earn and spend money freely and equally as all other Americans. In his "Letter," King says the following:

> Then came the opportunity last September to talk with some of the leaders of the economic community. In these negotiating sessions certain promises were made by the merchants—such as the promise to remove the humiliating racial signs from the stores. . . . As the weeks and months unfolded we realized that we were the victims of a broken promise. The signs remained. . . . We decided to set our direct action program around the Easter season, realizing that with the exception of Christmas, this was the largest shopping period of the year. Knowing that a strong economic withdrawal program would be the by-product of direct action, we felt that this was *the best time to bring pressure on the merchants* for the needed changes [emphasis added].[236]

Granting that there were many other noneconomic issues to be resolved, many of them only resolvable through the government, it remains the case that many other of the problems were, at their heart, economic matters. One of the most enduring symbols of the American civil rights movement was the lunch counter, another example of economic oppression. Still more vivid examples of extragovernmental civil disobedience arise in the context of more recent examples. These include, the logging, animal testing, and AIDS treatment controversies.

While groups associated with all of the aforementioned controversies employ lobbyists and governmentally centered activities, the most highly publicized and arguably most effective activities with regard to these issues surround such groups as Earth First!, People for the Ethical Treatment of Animals (PETA), and the AIDS Coalition to Unleash Power (ACT-UP). Actions such as tree spiking (hammering long metal spikes into trees and marking them as "spiked" such that when a saw hits the spike it destroys the saw blade), breaking into testing labs and releasing the test animals, and "zapping" the New York Stock Exchange are a few examples of what can be usefully described as company-directed civil disobedience that short-circuits the need for government action. While the government certainly held some threat of action in this case, it is more clearly the case that ACT-UP prompted the change in the pricing of AIDS treatments by what could be termed commercial civil disobedience. The government will continue to be the higher court for irreconcilable differences between business and activists, but an even higher court than the government is (ostensibly) that of public opinion, which is where activists have always made their greatest inroads.

Civil Disobedience and Stakeholder Theory

How, then, can the concept of civil disobedience aid in ethical analysis of stakeholders? Civilly disobedient social activists of the kind discussed here claim to represent some norm, already latent and accepted in society, that is not being appropriately adhered to within that same society. That is, by engaging in one of their "zaps," ACT-UP claims to represent some norm in the larger society to which, for example, Burroughs-Wellcome (B-W) was not adhering. Norms regarding (1) the value of human life versus recovery of expenses, (2) the morality of pricing to customers who are exceptionally desperate, and (3) the morality of pricing to customers who have no other alternatives are but a few of the possibilities for latent social norms that the activists perceive as not being adequately addressed by B-W. Conceived of as acts of civil disobedience, the actions of ACT-UP can be seen as communicating an intensely held moral belief that B-W was not properly abiding by an extant social norm.

When viewed in this way, civilly disobedient, social activist stakeholders should be treated as representatives of the larger society or community within which the corporation operates. Hence, even if the activists themselves are not considered normatively legitimate stakeholders (despite the fact that many of them are also customers), the revised civil disobedience model shows how they may be representatives of the local community, which is an archetypal stakeholder.

Conclusion

This chapter suggests some implications of a fairness-based stakeholder theory for stakeholder research. Among the uncertainties within stakeholder scholarship is the problem of stakeholder identity. This creates problems for stakeholder theory in that neither the scholar nor the manager has a method for determining to whom stakeholder obligations are due. As conceived by numerous scholars, stakeholder status may be granted to anyone and anything in an organization's environment and groups that merit stakeholder obligations proliferate without limit. Among the groups that have been posited as stakeholders are the natural environment and

activist interest groups. It was argued in this chapter that neither of these groups merit fairness-based stakeholder status,
but may nevertheless be derivative stakeholders in that they
can have some effect upon the other normative stakeholders.

In the case of stakeholder status for the natural environment, Starik's arguments regarding this subject were discussed
in light of the fairness-based view presented here. It was
argued that the natural environment is unable to undertake
the requisite obligation-generating activities to qualify as a
stakeholder. Nor is merely being affected (or less still, *potentially* being affected) by some individual or group action adequate for the creation of stakeholder obligations.

Another point of controversy among stakeholder theorists
is the stakeholder status of social activists. These groups, it is
argued, can clearly affect the organization, and as such, merit
stakeholder status on Freeman's original definition. This chapter argues that, with regard to both social activists and the natural environment, the mere ability to affect the organization
creates no more obligation on the part of the organization and
its managers than does a thug's ability to beat me up create a
moral obligation between us. Although activists and thugs can
affect, they are not owed moral consideration.

This does not imply, however, that the organization may
dismiss these entities as unimportant, because such entities are
still due moral consideration apart from stakeholder status
(e.g., as a person). The organization and its managers have
moral duties to both members of the activist groups and to the
natural environment apart from the stakeholder status of
these entities. These duties provide moral reasons prohibiting
certain rights-violating activities, but do not imply the additional moral obligations of normative stakeholder status.

Further, the concerns of and for activist groups and the
natural environment may also exist *within normative stakeholder
groups*, hence making these entities derivatively legitimate.
Thus, clean air and water are a concern of many within the

community of an organization (including its employees and other local stakeholders). As such, the organization has an obligation to consider the health of the local environment deriving from the stakeholder obligations owed to these normative stakeholder groups.

In the case of the social activist, the literature on civil disobedience is instructive in understanding the obligations between the organization and social activist groups. The civil disobediant claims that the object of protest is violating a community moral norm and may, as such, be considered a proxy for the local community. If the activist group does indeed represent a legitimate community concern, then the organization should engage in discourse with that group due to the stakeholder obligations to the local community.

CHAPTER 8

Stakeholder Theory in Practice

This book contains some rather dense prose and detailed arguments that are necessary for adding rigor to the theory. The theory does not, however, pass the "so what?" test unless it is—or can be made—useful to managers and administrators. In this concluding chapter, I will summarize the preceding arguments and encapsulate a few of the more practical managerial implications of the preceding discussion. These implications can be found throughout the book, but because they are easily lost when buried among the rest of the arguments, there is value in recapitulating some of the more prominent practical ideas in one place. I will do this by addressing some of the most common questions and challenges from students and business people. The questions often take the form of a progressive series.

- Why should managers pay attention to stakeholders?
- Who are an organization's stakeholders and what is the basis for their legitimacy?
- What do stakeholders want?
- How should managers prioritize among stakeholders?
- Are the ethics of business different from everyday ethics? If so, how and why?

This chapter will explicitly and concisely address these questions using the theory elaborated herein. Following this is a short list of books that the reader may wish to consult for assistance with the nuts and bolts of managing for stakeholders. The chapter will conclude with a brief discussion of some remaining challenges to stakeholder theory.

Why Should Managers Pay Attention to Stakeholders?

Perhaps the most fundamental challenge to stakeholder theory is establishing a justification for managerial attention to stakeholders akin to those justifying maximizing shareholder wealth.[237] This book has attempted to provide such a justification. Any convincing justification for maximizing shareholder wealth must, at its core, be a moral argument. The most convincing justification for maximizing shareholder wealth is the property rights argument popularized by Milton Friedman. Briefly, by virtue of owning equity shares, shareholders own the corporation. These owners wish to have the value of their investment maximized. Managers who fail to maximize shareholder wealth are not respecting this wish; they are spending, indeed stealing, another's money. This is a violation of a moral property right.[a]

In Chapter 4 and elsewhere I argued that positing share ownership as equivalent to ownership of the corporation does much of the heavy lifting in this argument, but is itself unjustified. Share owners own a right to a residual cash flow—a financial instrument. Ownership of equity shares implies ownership of the corporation no more than does owning any other financial instrument related to the corporation. The corporation is an independent entity that is "owned" by no one. No one speaks of "owning" a church, a university, or a nation. Certain individuals are responsible for the administration of these

---

[a]It may also be tantamount to socialism to Friedman, but this need not concern us here.

entities, but no one feels compelled to discern who owns them. Why should corporations be an exception? Without the concept of ownership, maximizing shareholder wealth also becomes a far less tenable proposition.

If the corporation and other organizations are to be considered entities unto themselves capable of bearing legal obligations, so too are they capable of bearing moral obligations. One such obligation is that of stakeholder fairness described in Chapter 5. By accepting the benefits of a mutually beneficial scheme of cooperation, organizations incur obligations to those who contribute. Part of this obligation is codified in the law, but much is not. From this perspective, shareholders are significant contributors and they are owed a significant obligation. This will typically take the form of dividends and an increase in the market value of the equity share in the case of well-run organizations. However, the obligation owed shareholders is only different in degree from that of other stakeholders, it is not different in kind. There is no special fiduciary obligation due shareholders, with other obligations being a lesser non-fiduciary variety. The obligations to all stakeholders are fairness based. Any fiduciary duties that exist run to the organization itself as an independent entity. Managers are the individuals responsible for administering the affairs of the organization including respecting the moral obligations entailed in the principle of stakeholder fairness. This is why managers must support the well-being of stakeholders as representatives of the organization.

Having convinced the skeptic that she should attend to stakeholders, but . . .

Who Are an Organization's Stakeholders and What Is the Basis for Their Legitimacy?

Since its inception, determining who is and who is not a stakeholder has been a point of some contention for the theory.

Should stakeholder status be narrowly construed and reserved only for those constituencies with some very close relationship with the organization? Or, should stakeholder status be broadly interpreted so as to account for the myriad groups who can affect and are affected by the organization? Are activists stakeholders? Competitors? The natural environment? The media? How are managers to decide?

The principle of stakeholder fairness provides a way of making this discernment. At a minimum, stakeholders are those groups from whom the organization has voluntarily accepted benefits. By doing so, the organization has incurred obligations of fairness to attend to the well-being of these stakeholders—at least insofar as their well-being is affected by interactions with the focal organization. This will typically include groups such as financiers, employees, customers, suppliers, and local communities.

What about the more controversial candidates for stakeholder status? Most organizations have not accepted benefits from their competitors or activist groups, but surely these groups would receive some consideration from a theory of strategic management. What does stakeholder theory say about the treatment of constituencies to whom it has no special obligation, but who can significantly influence the success of it and the stakeholders for whose well-being it is responsible? Here I distinguish between normatively and derivatively legitimate stakeholders. Some groups are legitimate stakeholders because they are owed an obligation. Others are stakeholders due to their abilities and likelihood of exerting influence over the organization and the stakeholders to whom it owes an obligation.

The effects that derivative stakeholders have may be either beneficial or harmful to the organization and its normative stakeholders. Competitors can certainly affect the organization and should therefore be considered legitimate stakeholders, but there is no moral obligation to attend to their well-being on the part of the organization and its managers. The media may help or harm the organization and its reputation among society and its customers, this does not make them part of the cooperative scheme. It is legitimate to expend resources managing the media, not for the sake of the media's intrinsic worth, but toward the end of advancing the goals of the organization. The natural environment is not a stakeholder, but normatively legitimate stakeholders may care deeply about the environment making it managerially legitimate to care for the natural environment. Stakeholder theory suggests that managers should be vigilant in uncovering stakeholders who may be sources of harm or benefit.

Now we know how to figure out who the stakeholders are, but . . .

What Do Stakeholders Want?

Many stakeholder groups are not satisfied with simply being allocated some measure of organizational value; they want a say in how the organization creates this value. Perhaps not all, but many stakeholders want some voice in organizational decision making. Those who desire a voice should have it.

This book has consistently prescribed that managing for stakeholders involves managerial attention to their well-being. Too often, however, managers sit in an office among themselves and try to divine what stakeholders want from their relationship with the organization. Someone in human resources is responsible for discerning or representing what employees want; someone in public relations conveys the desires of the local community to other managers. Stakeholder maps are drawn and managers *assume* stakeholders' desires. Stakeholder interaction and discourse is not simply the purview of localized specialized departments but is the responsibility of managers at all levels throughout the organization.

This call for a stakeholder communication is not unique to this work. It is the foundation for "management by walking around" popularized by Peters and Waterman in *In Search of Excellence*[238] and has been a significant feature in too many other managerial approaches to list. Although not new, the significance of stakeholder communication finds some additional support here. Stakeholder communication is not only good for the organization, but also is a matter of moral obligation. Those who contribute to the organization should be permitted some say in how that organization is managed. Managers in continuous contact with stakeholders are in a better position to cooperatively determine organizational goals, take advantage of unforeseen but mutually advantageous opportunities (e.g., cost reductions throughout the supply chain), and perhaps avoid conflict before it reaches critical mass (e.g., communication with dissatisfied employees or activists).

Of note, advocating stakeholder communication does not imply organizational democracy or stakeholder boards of directors or any other specific institutional structure—nor does it rule them out. How a particular company creates and reinforces stakeholder dialog is best left to the managers and stakeholders themselves. The important point is that communication be frequent and as thorough as possible.

Now we know how to discover what stakeholders want from the organization.

However, we live in a world of scarce resources, so . . .

How Should Managers Prioritize among Stakeholders?

Another issue that has historically plagued stakeholder theory is how managers should allocate their limited time, attention, mental capacity, and other scarce resources among stakeholders. While there is no determinate algorithm for making such decisions, the stakeholder theory defended here does imply some broad direction for such prioritizing. Normative stakeholders take moral precedence over derivative stakeholders. This is obvious from the fact that concern for derivative stake-

holders is only justified by reference to normative stakeholders. Certainly a manager should know what the stakeholders
believe to be in their best interests prior to trying to make this
happen. This normative/derivative distinction provides for
one sort of priority.

Complicating the matter, however, is the fact that advancing the interests of the organization and its normative stakeholders may involve spending a lot of time and resources
attending to the demands of derivative stakeholders—and this
may be with the blessing of the normatively legitimate stakeholders. If some activist group or competitor threatens the viability of the organization, managers should exert as much time
and effort as necessary dealing with this threat. Such trade-offs
would likely be acceptable to other stakeholders as long as it is
understood to be in their interest and the interest of the
organization.

This is an important point about priority. There are many
ways of translating the concept of priority. For most people,
time at work necessarily implies time away from family; but this
need not imply a prioritization of work over family. For many,
time at work makes time with their family possible—even if the
time at work exceeds the number of waking hours spent with
one's family during a particular time period. The individual's
priority still lies with the family, but measuring time spent on
work against time spent with the family would be a misleading
indicator of this hierarchy.

Staying with the analogy to the family for a moment, it may
also bear mention that a person who continually claims to be
working for the family, but fails to spend *any* time with them—
moving from one work crisis to another—could justifiably have
some doubt cast upon her claims. So too with managers. Managing for stakeholders may involve spending the bulk of time
and resources contending with the issues raised by derivative
stakeholders *for a limited period.* Managers who do not devote
such resources to stakeholders for an extended period may

reasonably find their commitment to stakeholder management cast into doubt. Keeping the ideas in this book in mind may help managers better recall for whose benefit they are (or should be) managing the organization.

There is one final way that the stakeholder theory defended here can provide some managerial guidance in prioritizing stakeholders. As elaborated in Chapter 2, many stakeholder critics (and some advocates) have interpreted the concept of "balancing" stakeholder interests as implying that all stakeholders should be treated equally. According to the principle of stakeholder fairness, stakeholders should have a slice of the organizational outputs and a voice in how value is added by the organization that is consistent with their contributions to the organization. In other words, balance does not imply equality of voice or share of outputs. Voice and share—and therefore a sort of priority—should be based on contribution to the organization. The more a stakeholder group contributes to the organization, the greater their voice and share of value created should be.

Both inputs and outcomes are however typically incommensurate. How a manager is to evaluate the relative contributions of financier capital, employee effort and expertise, and customer loyalty in making allocation decisions bears no easy prescription. This is among the least quantitatively tractable questions of administration and a significant part of the *art* of management. That said, there is at least some direction provided by the prescription of equitability (rather than equality) as the criterion of distribution. As with prioritization based on the source of legitimacy, the criterion of equity provides no precise algorithm. Managers are, however, provided with some broad target at which to aim. Finally . . .

Are the Ethics of Business Different from Everyday Ethics?

Another managerial implication of this discussion of stakeholder theory is its contribution to the question of the distinctiveness of business ethics from ordinary, everyday ethics. Commentators and many managers alike have suggested that the ethics of business are of a less strict variety than the ethics that pervade day-to-day life. Albert Z. Carr's polemic of more than thirty years ago sums up this belief. In comparing the ethics of business to the ethics of poker he writes:

> Poker's own brand of ethics is different from the ethical ideals of civilized human relationships. The game calls for distrust of the other fellow. It ignores the claim of friendship. Cunning deception and concealment of one's strength and intentions, not kindness and openheartedness, are vital in poker. No one thinks any the worse of poker on that account. And no one should think any the worse of the game of business because its standards of right and wrong differ from the prevailing traditions of morality in our society.[239]

In addition to the large segment of the world that, with some cause, believes the ethics of business are of a lesser grade than those of the rest of society, some defend the notion that this *should be* the case. I defend precisely the opposite contention here.

As has been repeatedly emphasized throughout, stakeholder obligations do not replace, but are *in addition to* the duties that existed prior to organizational scheme of cooperation. Running an organization does not license a manager to violate the norms and standards of society but instead presents a brand new set of moral considerations based on stakeholder obligations. At least with regard to normatively legitimate stakeholders,[b] the ethics of business are slightly different from those of civil society, but not in the way that Carr envisions. Obligations are added rather than diminished.

---

[b]I shall not undertake a point-by-point critique of Carr's position, but it does bear reiteration that the additional moral obligations described are owed to the normatively legitimate stakeholders (e.g., financiers, employees, customers) and are not necessarily owed to derivatively legitimate stakeholders (e.g., competitors). Carr's suggestion that "bluffing" is merely part of business may be true in some limited contexts, but those situations are far less common and general than he indicates.

Stakeholder Best Practice

Hopefully, managers having read this remain dissatisfied with the conclusions. This dissatisfaction also would hopefully lead to the deeper examination, reflection, and study of managing for stakeholders in particular contexts. If so, additional books can direct managers for more practical advice on this topic. None are entirely satisfactory, but together they present a picture of global best practice in managing for stakeholders.

Though currently out of print, Freeman's groundbreaking book, *Strategic Management: A Stakeholder Approach*, still presents a lucid and informative framework for stakeholder management including examples and vignettes from his experience as a consultant. It certainly merits a visit to the catalog of the library.

Other sources of specific how-to information and lengthy discussions of the practices and techniques used by other companies include the following:

- Ann Svendsen, 1998, *The Stakeholder Strategy: Profiting from Collaborative Business Relationships* (San Francisco: Berrett-Koehler Publishers).
- David Wheeler & Maria Sillanpää, 1997, *The Stakeholder Corporation: A Blueprint for Maximizing Stakeholder Value* (London: Pitman Publishing).
- James E. Post, Lee E. Preston, & Sybille Sachs, 2002, *Redefining the Corporation: Stakeholder Management and Organizational Wealth* (Stanford, CA: Stanford University Press).

Reflective managers may find these works helpful and use them with other resources and experiences to craft their own approach to stakeholder management.

Other Challenges to Stakeholder Theory

It is the height of hubris to believe that one has had the last word on anything, so undoubtedly this is not the final statement of stakeholder theory, primarily because difficulties remain with the theory even under the most generous and coherent interpretations. In this section I suggest a number of areas where the theory remains in need of further elaboration or defense. Knowledge of these weaknesses can hopefully motivate future study, elaboration, and amendment of the theory.

As suggested, stakeholder theory falls victim to some criticisms in no greater degree than alternative conceptions (e.g., the shareholder wealth maximization view). I argued, for example, that managerial opportunism represents no greater threat to stakeholder theory than to the alternatives. That said, however, managerial opportunism still represents a threat to organizational effectiveness under any current approach. Work proceeds apace—under the rubrics of the theory of the firm, agency theory, and transaction cost economics among others—on the question of how best to minimize managerial opportunism within a shareholder wealth maximization regime. Similar work might well be undertaken from the perspective of stakeholder theory. Indeed, the tools and concepts employed under the rubric of agency theory could be usefully applied within a stakeholder theoretical framework once the connotations of corporate ownership described earlier are clarified and rectified.

It would be tempting to place the question of adjudicating between stakeholder demands in the same category. While no more a problem for normative stakeholder theory (i.e., managing in stakeholder's interests for reasons intrinsic to the stakeholders themselves) than for instrumental stakeholder theory (i.e., managing stakeholder interests to maximize the outcomes of another) or shareholder wealth maximization theory, it is tempting to say that adjudicating between stakeholder interests is another problem in need of *ex ante* solution. This is not especially problematic, however, for either stakeholder theory or the alternatives. The "corporate veil" and "business judgment rule" are not necessary evils, but positive contributions to the spirit of pragmatic experimentalism. *Ex ante* rules for deriving a hierarchy of stakeholders—in the abstract—is as misguided in stakeholder theory as is the presumption of the dominion of shareholders. Managing for stakeholders, indeed all top-level strategic management, is organic in its nature. Management is more art than science. As much as we may believe that we want a definite heuristic for management, one is neither available nor likely even desirable.

That said, there may be a potentially more damaging aspect to the question of stakeholder adjudication. Those who argue for a narrow conception of stakeholders argue for the importance of distinguishing between stakeholders and non-stakeholders. The earlier argument suggesting that stakeholder theory should not be considered a comprehensive moral scheme suggests that managers will also face conflicts between stakeholder and non-stakeholder issues. Orts and Strudler[240] examine the relationship between stakeholder theory and the natural environment and conclude that stakeholder theory cannot account for duties to non-humans (see Chapter 7 for a discussion of the stakeholder status of the natural environment). This leads to the question of how obligations to stakeholders should be weighed against other moral duties to non-stakeholders. This is rather similar to the question that stakeholder theorists ask of shareholder wealth maximization advocates with different in-groups and out-groups and stands in need of some elaboration.

Little has also been written about the role of "community" as stakeholder—surely the most controversial of customer, supplier, employee, financier and community. Berman, Wicks, Kotha, and Jones[241] found no significant effect between community relations and financial performance. Orts and Strudler's version of stakeholder theory "denies that government and members of the community in which it [the firm] operates must be regarded as stakeholders, even if their economic interests are affected by the firm."[242] Systematic ambiguity in the notion of "community" has recently been explored,[243] but much work remains.

Indeed, the improvement of organizational management is a pursuit with no end. There is no one right way to run a business, a nation, or a life. We must recognize that the instrumental and prudential aspects of this pursuit are two sides of the same coin. Using stakeholder theory as a framework for organizational administration keeps the morality of management foremost in our minds as we seek to continually improve our methods of creating value.

NOTES

[1]John Rawls, 1971, *A Theory of Justice* (Cambridge, MA: The Belknap Press of Harvard University Press), p. viii.

[2]K. E. Goodpaster, 1991, "Business Ethics and Stakeholder Analysis," *Business Ethics Quarterly,* 1(1), p. 63.

[3]Michael C. Jensen, 2000, "Value Maximization and the Corporate Objective Function," in M. Beer & N. Nohria, *Breaking the Code of Change* (Boston: Harvard Business School Press), pp. 37–58. Reprinted as (2002) Value Maximization, Stakeholder Theory, and the Corporate Objective Function, *Business Ethics Quarterly,* 12(2), pp. 235–256. See also Donaldson & Preston, 1995; Jones, 1995; Sternberg, 2000.

[4]O. E. Williamson, & J. Bercovitz, 1996, "The Modern Corporation as an Efficiency Instrument: The Comparative Contracting Perspective," in C. Kaysen (ed.), *The American Corporation Today* (New York: Oxford University Press), pp. 327–359. See also Elaine Sternberg, 2001, The Stakeholder Concept: A Mistaken Doctrine, Foundation for Business Responsibilities; Sternberg, 2000, *Just Business* (New York: Oxford University Press); Sternberg, 1998, *Corporate Governance: Accountability in the Marketplace* (London: The Institute of Economic Affairs); Jensen, 2000.

[5]Michael Hammer & James Champy, 1993, *Reengineering the Corporation* (New York: HarperBusiness).

[6]Jones & Wicks, 1999a.

[7]Jeff Frooman, 1999, "Stakeholder Influence Strategies," *Academy of Management Review,* 24(2): 191–205; J. Pfeffer, & G. Salancik, 1978, *The External Control of Organizations* (New York: Harper and Row).

[8]This categorization emerged during correspondence with Joshua Margolis.

[9]Cf. G. G. Sollars, 2001, "An Appraisal of Shareholder Proportional Liability" *Journal of Business Ethics,* 32(4), pp. 329–345.

[10]See also, Orts, 1997.

[11]Alexei M Marcoux, 2000, "Balancing Act" in J. R. DesJardins, & J. J. McCall (eds.), *Contemporary Issues in Business Ethics,* 4th ed.,(Wadsworth), p. 97 (Marcoux's emphasis.)

[12]Sternberg, 2000, p. 51f.

[13]Albert J. Dunlap, 1996, *Mean Business* (New York: Simon & Schuster); John A. Byrne, 1999, *Chainsaw* (New York: HarperBusiness).

[14]"Former Sunbeam Chief Exec Settles Hldr Lawsuit for $15M," Dow Jones Newswire, January 14, 2002.

[15]Hill & Jones, 1992.

[16]*Ibid.,* p. 145.

[17]Charles Handy, 1992, "Balancing Corporate Power: A New Federalist Paper," *Harvard Business Review,* Nov-Dec, pp. 59–67.

[18]Sternberg, 2000, p. 51.

[19]Marcoux, 2000.

[20]Jensen, 2000, p. 49.

[21]*Ibid.,* p. 42.

[22]Donaldson & Dunfee, 1999, p. 262. (Emphasis added.)

[23]Jason A. Colquitt, Donald E. Conlon, Michael J. Wesson, Christopher O. L. H. Porter, & K. Yee Ng, 2001, "Justice at the Millennium: A Meta–Analytic Review of 25 Years of Organizational Justice Research," *Journal of Applied Psychology,* 86(3), pp. 425–445; Jerald Greenberg, 1990a, Employee Theft as a Reaction to Underpayment Inequity: The Hidden Cost of Pay Cuts, *Journal of Applied Psychology,* 75(5), pp. 561–568; Jerald Greenberg, 1990b, "Organizational Justice: Yesterday, Today, and Tomorrow,"*Journal of Management,* 16(2), pp. 399–432.

[24]E. A. Lind & T. Tyler, 1988, *The Social Psychology of Procedural Justice* (New York: Plenum).

[25]J. S. Adams, 1963,"Toward an Understanding of Inequity," *Journal of Abnormal and Social Psychology,* 67, pp. 422–436.

[26]D. A. Gioia, 1999, "Practicability, Paradigms, and Problems in Stakeholder Theorizing," *Academy of Management Review,* 24(2), pp. 228–232. See also Marcoux, 2000; Sternberg, 2000; cf., Jones & Wicks, 1999b.

[27]David A. Nadler & Michael L. Tushman, 1997, *Competing by Design: The Power of Organizational Architecture* (New York: Oxford University Press).

[28]Sloan Stakeholder Colloquy, 1999, "Clarkson Principles," http://mgmt.utoronto.ca/~stake/Principles.htm The Sloan Stakeholder Colloquy was a broad and important effort to promote and organize research on issues surrounding stakeholder theory. (Emphasis added.)

[29]Sternberg, 2000, p. 50.

[30]Deutsch, 1975, 1985; Elster, 1992; Leventhal, 1976; Walzer, 1983.

[31]Deutsch, 1975, p. 145.

[32]Greenberg, 1990, p. 401.

[33]Deutsch, 1985.

[34]Marens & Wicks, 1999.

[35]Orts, 1992, 1997.

[36]Jensen, 2000; Williamson & Bercovitz, 1996.

[37]John Hendry, 2001a, "Missing the Target: Normative Stakeholder Theory and the Corporate Governance Debate," *Business Ethics Quarterly,* 11(1), pp. 159–176; John Hendry, 2001b, "Economic Contracts versus Social Relationships as a Foundation for Normative Stakeholder Theory,"*Business Ethics: A European Review,* 10(3), pp. 223–232; Harry J. Van Buren, III, 2001, "If Fairness Is the Problem, Is Consent the Solution? Integrating ISCT and Stakeholder Theory," *Business Ethics Quarterly,* 11(3), pp. 481–500.

[38]Collins & Porras, 1994.

[39]T. J. Peters & R. H. Waterman, 1982, *In Search of Excellence* (New York: Harper & Row).

[40]P. M. Senge, 1990, *The Fifth Discipline* (New York: Doubleday).

[41]R. Edward Freeman & Robert A. Phillips, 2002, "Stakeholder Theory: A Libertarian Defense," *Business Ethics Quarterly,* 12(3), pp. 331–349.

[42]Anthony Barnett, 1997, "Towards a Stakeholder Democracy," in Gavin Kelly, Dominic Kelly, & Andrew Gamble (eds.), *Stakeholder Capitalism* (London: MacMillan Press), pp. 82–98; Will Hutton, 1995, *The State We're In* (London: Jonathan Cape); Mike Rustin, 1997, "Stakeholding and the Public

Sector," in Gavin Kelly, Dominic Kelly, & Andrew Gamble (eds.), *Stakeholder Capitalism* (London: MacMillan Press), pp. 72–81.

[43]Dan Corry, 1997, "Macroeconomic Policy and Stakeholder Capitalism," in Gavin Kelly, Dominic Kelly, & Andrew Gamble (eds.), *Stakeholder Capitalism* (London: MacMillan Press), pp. 185–202.

[44]Jonathan Perraton, 1997, "The Global Economy," in Gavin Kelly, Dominic Kelly, & Andrew Gamble (eds.), *Stakeholder Capitalism* (London: MacMillan Press), pp. 226–237.

[45]*Ibid.*, 1997, p. 232.

[46]David Soskice, 1997, "Stakeholding Yes; the German Model No," in Gavin Kelly, Dominic Kelly, & Andrew Gamble (eds.), *Stakeholder Capitalism* (London: MacMillan Press), pp. 219–225.

[47]*Ibid.*, p. 223.

[48]Kelly, Kelly, & Gamble, 1997, p. 249

[49]Orts (1997) traces scholarly interest in "intermediate associations" back to German sociologist Johannes Althusius, 1614/1964, *The Politics of Johannes Althusius*, Frederick S. Carney (trans.).

[50]Orts & Strudler, 2002.

[51]Donaldson & Dunfee, 1999, pp. 246f

[52]A. B. Carroll, 1991, "The Pyramid of Corporate Social Responsibility: Toward the Moral Management of Organizational Stakeholders," *Business Horizons,* 34(4), 39–48.

[53]Orts, 1997, p. 175.

[54]1995: 72, emphasis added.

[55]This chapter is based largely upon an article I coauthored with Joshua Margolis in *Business Ethics Quarterly* 9(4) entitled, "Toward an Ethics of Organizations." Professor Margolis should not be held responsible for the amplifications or alterations in the present chapter not found in the original article.

[56]John Rawls, 1999, "The Independence of Moral Theory," in Samuel Freeman (ed.), *Collected Papers,* (Cambridge, MA: Harvard University Press), p. 302.

[57]Edwin M. Hartman, 1996, *Organizational Ethics and the Good Life* (New York: Oxford University Press), p. 7.

[58]T. Donaldson, & T. W. Dunfee, 1999, *Ties That Bind* (Boston: Harvard Business School Press); Donaldson & Dunfee, 1995, "Integrative Social Contracts Theory: A Communitarian Conception of Economic Ethics," *Economics and Philosophy,* 11, pp. 85–112; Donaldson & Dunfee, 1994, "Toward a Unified Conception of Business Ethics: Integrative Social Contracts Theory," *Academy of Management Review,* 18(2), pp. 252–284; Hartman, *ibid.* 1996; Hartman, 2001, "Moral Philosophy, Political Philosophy, and Organizational Ethics: A Response to Phillips and Margolis," *Business Ethics Quarterly,* 11(4), pp. 673–686: Robert C. Solomon, 1993, *Ethics and Excellence: Cooperation and Integrity in Business* (New York: Oxford University Press).

[59]Donaldson & Dunfee, 1994, 1995, 1999; Michael Keeley, 1988, *A Social Contract Theory of Organizations* (Notre Dame: University of Notre Dame Press).

[60]Hartman, 1996; Solomon, 1993.

[61]T. L. Fort, 1996, "Business as Mediating Institution," *Business Ethics Quarterly,* 6(2), 149–163.

[62]Edwin M. Hartman, 1994, "The Commons and the Moral Organization," *Business Ethics Quarterly,* 4(3), pp. 253–269.

[63]R. Edward Freeman, 1994, "The Politics of Stakeholder Theory: Some Future Directions," *Business Ethics Quarterly,* 4(4), pp. 409–422.

[64]Hartman, 1996.

[65]Donaldson & Dunfee, 1994, 1995, 1999.

[66]John Rawls, 1993, *Political Liberalism* (New York: Columbia University Press); John Rawls, 1971, *A Theory of Justice* (Cambridge, MA: The Belknap Press of Harvard University Press).

[67]Freeman, 1994; Hartman, 1996; Carroll U. Stephens, Virginia W. Gerde, Richard E. Wokutch, & George Watson, 1997, "The Value-Rational Organization: A Rawlsian Perspective on Structure," paper presented at the 1997 Annual Meeting of the International Association of Business and Society.

[68]Rawls, 1993, p. 14.

[69]*Ibid.*, 1993, p. 40ff

[70]*Ibid.*, 1993, p. 277.

[71]John Rawls, 1971, "Justice as Reciprocity," in *Collected Papers*, 1999 (Cambridge, MA: Harvard University Press), p. 190.

[72]M. Deutsch, 1975, "Equity, Equality, and Need: What Determines Which Value Will Be Used As the Basis for Distributive Justice?" *Journal of Social Issues*, 31(3), pp. 137–149; Deutsch, 1985, *Distributive Justice* (New Haven: Yale University Press); G. S. Leventhal, 1980, "What Should Be Done with Equity Theory? New Approaches to the Study of Fairness in Social Relationships," in K. Gergen, M. Greenberg, & R. Willis (eds.), *Social Exchange: Advances in Theory and Research* (New York: Plenum Press), pp. 27–55; G. S. Leventhal, J. Karuza, & W. R. Fry, 1980, "Beyond Fairness: A Theory of Allocation Preferences," in G. Mikula (ed.), *Justice and Social Interaction* (New York: Springer–Verlag), pp. 167–218; G. S. Leventhal, 1976, "The Distribution of Rewards and Resources in Groups and Organizations," in L. Berkowitz & E. Walster (eds.), *Advances in Experimental Social Psychology*, Vol. 9 (New York: Academic Press), pp. 91–131.

[73]Kenneth Arrow, Samuel Bowles, & Steven Durlauf (eds.), 2000, *Meritocracy and Economic Inequality* (Princeton, NJ: Princeton University Press); Michael Young, 1958, *The Rise of the Meritocracy* (London: Thames and Hudson); Norman Daniels, 1978, "Merit and Meritocracy," *Philosophy and Public Affairs*, 3: pp 206–223; A. Donnellon & M. Scully, 1994, "Teams, Performance, and Rewards," in C. Hecksher & A. Donnellon (eds.), *The Post-Bureaucratic Organization* (Thousand Oaks, CA: Sage Publications), pp. 63–89.

[74]Hartman, 1996, 2001.

[75]Michael Sandel, 1982, *Liberalism and the Limits of Justice* (Cambridge: Cambridge University Press).

[76]Norman Daniels (ed.), 1989, *Reading Rawls* (Stanford, CA: Stanford University Press); Ronald Dworkin, 1973, "The Original Position," *University of Chicago Law Review*, 40(3), pp. 500–533; Milton Fisk, 1989, "History and Reason in Rawls' Moral Theory," in Norman Daniels (ed.), *Reading Rawls* (Stanford, CA: Stanford University Press), pp. 53–80; Thomas Nagel, 1973, "Rawls on Justice," *Philosophical Review*, 82(2), pp. 220–234.

[77]Michael Walzer, 1994, *Thick and Thin* (Notre Dame, IN: University of Notre Dame Press).

[78]Donaldson & Dunfee, 1999, 1995, 1994.

[79]*Ibid.*, 1999.

[80]Walzer, 1994.

[81]Donaldson & Dunfee, 1995, p. 86. In a later section an answer to Donaldson & Dunfee's criticism of stakeholder theory is provided.

[82]*Ibid.*, p. 90.

[83]See James G. March and Herbert A. Simon, 1958, *Organizations*, 2nd ed. (Cambridge, MA: Blackwell).

[84]John Dewey, 1957, *Reconstruction in Philosophy* (Boston: Beacon Press).

[85]Amartya Sen, 2000, "Merit and Justice," in Kenneth Arrow, Samuel Bowles, & Steven Durlauf (eds.), *Meritocracy and Economic Inequality* (Princeton, NJ: Princeton University Press), p. 5.

[86]James C. Collins & Jerry I. Porras, 1994, *Built to Last: Successful Habits of Visionary Companies* (New York: Harper Collins).

[87]D. A. Schon, 1983, *The Reflective Practitioner: How Professionals Think in Action* (New York: Basic Books).

[88]Joshua D. Margolis, 1998, *Dignity in the Balance: Philosophical and Practical Dimensions of Promoting Ethics in Organizations,* Ph.D. dissertation, Harvard University.

[89]Solomon makes a similar point regarding the need for positive goals from the perspective of virtue ethics (Solomon, 1993).

[90]R. Edward Freeman & Robert A. Phillips, 2002, "Libertarian Stakeholder Theory," *Business Ethics Quarterly,* 12(3), pp. 331–349.

[91]See R. Edward Freeman, April 1997, "Political Philosophy, As if Business Matters" presented at the 25th Conference on Value Inquiry.

[92]John Rawls, 1999, "The Independence of Moral Theory," in Samuel Freeman (ed.), *Collected Papers* (Cambridge, MA: Harvard University Press), p. 287.

[93]*Ibid.,* p. 302.

[94]Elizabeth Anderson, 1993, *Values in Ethics and Economics* (Cambridge, MA: Harvard University Press); Amartya Sen, 1987, *On Ethics and Economics* (Oxford: Basil Blackwell).

[95]Lionel Robbins, 1935, *An Essay on the Nature and Significance of Economic Science* (London: Macmillan).

[96]Amartya Sen, 1987, *On Ethics and Economics* (Cambridge, MA: Blackwell), p. 2.

[97]See Andrea Gabor, 2000, *The Capitalist Philosophers* (New York: Times Business), p. 22.

[98]See Jay M. Shafritz & J. Steven Ott (eds.), 2001, *Classics of Organization Theory,* 5th ed. (Fort Worth: Harcourt College Publishers).

[99]Mary Parker Follett, 1995, *Mary Parker Follett–Prophet of Management,* Pauline Graham (ed.) (Boston: Harvard Business School Press).

[100]Chester Barnard, 1938/1968, *The Functions of the Executive* (Cambridge, MA: Harvard University Press).

[101]Joshua Margolis & James P. Walsh, "Misery Loves Companies: Whither Social Initiatives by Business?" unpublished manuscript; 2001, *People and Profits? The Search for a Link Between a Company's Social and Financial Performance* (Mahwah, NJ: Lawrence Erlbaum).

[102]*Ibid.;* 2001, p. 38.

[103]Phillip E. Tetlock, 2000, "Cognitive Biases and Organizational Correctives: Do Both Disease and Cure Depend on the Politics of the Beholder?" *Administrative Science Quarterly,* 45(2), pp. 293–326.

[104]*Ibid.,* p. 323.

[105]Thomas M. Jones & Andrew C. Wicks, 1999a, "Convergent Stakeholder Theory," *Academy of Management Review,* 24(2), pp. 206–221.

[106]Thomas Donaldson & L.E. Preston, 1995, "The Stakeholder Theory of the Corporation: Concepts, Evidence, and Implications," *Academy of Management Review,* 20(1), pp. 65–91.

[107]See R. Edward Freeman, 1996, "Understanding Stakeholder Capitalism," *Financial Times* (London Edition), July 18; Robert Kuttner, 1996, "High Stakes Capitalism," *The Washington Post,* April 8, p. A21; "Shareholder Values," *The Economist,* February 10, 1996, pp. 15–16; "Stakeholder Capitalism," *The Economist,* February 10, 1996, pp. 23–25; Gavin Kelly, Dominic Kelly, & Andrew Gamble (eds.), 1997, *Stakeholder Capitalism* (New York: St. Martin's

Press); Sloan Stakeholder Colloquy, http://www.mgmt.utoronto.ca/~stake/ web site; Clarkson Center for Business Ethics, 1999, "Principles of Stakeholder Management: The Clarkson Principles" (Toronto: The Clarkson Center for Business Ethics).

[108]Timothy J. Rowley, 1997, "Moving Beyond Dyadic Ties: A Network Theory of Stakeholder Influences," *Academy of Management Review* 22(4), pp. 887–910.

[109]Jeff Frooman, 1999, "Stakeholder Influence Strategies," *Academy of Management Review,* 24(2), pp 191–205.

[110]See, for example, Shawn L. Berman, Andrew C. Wicks, Suresh Kotha, & Thomas M. Jones, 1999, "Does Stakeholder Orientation Matter? The Relationship Between Stakeholder Management Models and Firm Financial Performance," *Academy of Management Journal,* 42(5), pp. 488–506; Stuart Ogden & Robert Watson, 1999, "Corporate Performance and Stakeholder Management: Balancing Shareholder and Customer Interests in the U.K. Privatized Water Industry," *Academy of Management Journal,* 42(5), pp 526–538.

[111]Eric Orts, 1997, "A North American Legal Perspective on Stakeholder Management Theory," *Perspectives on Company Law,* 2, pp. 165–179; Orts, 1992, "Beyond Shareholders: Interpreting Corporate Constituency Statutes," *George Washington Law Review,* 61, pp. 14–135.

[112]Orts, 1992.

[113]The following list is but a sample providing the interested reader a place to begin: A. A. Berle Jr., 1931, "Corporate Powers as Powers in Trust, *Harvard Law Review,* 44; A. A. Berle Jr., 1932, "For Whom Corporate Managers are Trustees, "*Harvard Law Review,* 45; John Carter, 1992, "The Rights of Other Corporate Constituencies," *Memphis State Law Review* 22; John C. Coffee Jr., 1986, "Shareholders versus Managers: The Strain in the Corporate Web, " *Michigan Law Review,* 85; Deborah A. DeMott, 1988, "Beyond Metaphor: An Analysis of Fiduciary Obligation," *Duke Law Journal;* E. Merrick Dodd, Jr., 1932, "For Whom Are Corporate Managers Are Trustees?" *Harvard Law Review,* 45; Timothy L. Fort, 1995, "Corporate Constituency Statutes: A Dialectical Interpretation," *Journal of Law and Commerce,* 15, pp. 257–294; Wai Shun Wilson Leung, 1997, "The Inadequacy of Shareholder Primacy: A Proposed Corporate Regime that Recognizes Non-Shareholder Interests," *Columbia J. of Law and Social Problems,* 30; Jonathan R. Macey, 1999, "Fiduciary Duties as Residual Claims: Obligations to Nonshareholder Constituencies from a Theory of the Firm Perspective," *Cornell Law Review,* 84, pp. 1266–1281; Jonathan R. Macey, 1991, "An Economic Analysis of the Various Rationales for Making Shareholders the Exclusive Beneficiaries of Corporate Fiduciary Duties," *Stetson Law Review,* 21; Jonathan R. Macey & G. P. Miller, 1993, "Corporate Stakeholders: A Contractual Perspective," University of Toronto Law Review, 43; Morey McDaniel, 1991, "Stockholders and Stakeholders," *Stetson Law Review* 21; David Millon, 1991, "Redefining Corporate Law," *Indiana Law Review,* 24; Lawrence E. Mitchell, 1992, "A Theoretical and Practical Framework for Enforcing Corporate Constituency Statutes," *Texas Law Review,* 70; Terry A. O'Neill, 1993, "Employees' Duty of Loyalty and the Corporate Constituency Debate," *Connecticut Law Review,* 25, pp. 681–716; Lewis D. Solomon, 1990, "Humanistic Economics: A New Model for the Corporate Constituency Debate," *U. of Cincinnati Law Review,* 59; A. A. Sommer, Jr. 1991, "Whom Should the Corporation Serve? The Berle–Dodd Debate Revisited Sixty Years Later," *Delaware Journal of Corporate Law,* 16; Katherine Van Wezel Stone, 1991, "Employees as Stakeholders Under State Nonshareholder Constituency Statutes," *Stetson Law Review* 21(1); Mark E. Van Der Weide, 1996, "Against Fiduciary Duties to Corporate

Stakeholders," *Delaware Journal of Corporate Law;* Gary von Strange, 1995, "Corporate Social Responsibility Through Constituency Statutes: Legend or Lie?" *Hofstra Labor Law Journal,* 11(2), pp. 461–497; Steven M. H. Wallman, 1991, "The Proper Interpretation of Corporate Constituency Statutes and Formulation of Director Duties," *Stetson Law Review,* 21.

[114]J. Thompson, 1967, *Organizations in Action* (New York: McGraw Hill).

[115]Freeman, 1984, p. 46.

[116]Ronald K. Mitchell, Bradley R. Agle, & Donna J. Wood, 1997, "Toward a Theory of Stakeholder Identification and Salience: Defining the Principle of Who and What Really Counts," *Academy of Management Review,* 22(4), p. 854.

[117]Thomas Donaldson & L. E. Preston, 1995, "The Stakeholder Theory of the Corporation: Concepts, Evidence, and Implications," *Academy of Management Review,* 20(1), pp. 65–91.

[118]T. M. Jones, & A. C. Wicks, 1999a, "Convergent Stakeholder Theory," *Academy of Management Review,* 24(2)pp. 206–221.

[119]R. E. Freeman, 1999, "Divergent Stakeholder Theory," *Academy of Management Review,* 24(2),pp. 233–236.

[120]*Ibid.,* p. 234.

[121]This became clear to me during a conversation with Shawn Berman.

[122]The roots of agency theory in economics are typically traced to E. F. Fama, 1980, "Agency Problems and the Theory of the Firm," *Journal of Political Economy,* 88, pp. 288–307; E. F. Fama & M. C. Jensen, 1983, "Separation of Ownership and Control," *Journal of Law and Economics,* 26, pp. 301–325; E. F. Fama & M. C. Jensen, 1983, "Agency Problems and Residual Claims," *Journal of Law and Economics,* 26, pp. 327–349; M. C. Jensen & W. H. Meckling, 1976, "Theory of the Firm: Managerial Behavior, Agency Costs, and Ownership Structure," *Journal of Financial Economics,* 3, pp. 305–360.

[123]C. W. L. Hill & T. M. Jones, 1992, "Stakeholder-Agency Theory," *Journal of Management Studies,* 29, pp. 131–154; Ian Maitland, 1994, "The Morality of the Corporation: An Empirical or Normative Disagreement?" *Business Ethics Quarterly,* 4(4), pp. 445–458; Dennis P. Quinn & Thomas M. Jones, 1995, "An Agent Morality View of Business Policy," *Academy of Management Review,* 20(1), pp. 22–42; Neil A. Shankman, 1996, "Reframing the Debate Between Agency and Stakeholder Theories of the Firm," *Journal of Business Ethics,* 19, pp. 319–334; A. Sharplin & L. D. Phelps, 1989, "A Stakeholder Apologetic for Management," *Business and Professional Ethics Journal,* 8(2), pp. 41–53.

[124]K. E. Goodpaster, 1991, "Business Ethics and Stakeholder Analysis," *Business Ethics Quarterly,* 1(1), pp. 53–73; John R. Boatright, 1994, "What's So Special About Shareholders," *Business Ethics Quarterly,* 4(4), pp. 393–408.

[125]William M. Evan & R. Edward Freeman, 1993, "A Stakeholder Theory of the Modern Corporation: Kantian Capitalism," in Tom L. Beauchamp & Norman E. Bowie (eds.), *Ethical Theory and Business,* 4th ed. (Englewood Cliffs, NJ: Prentice Hall).

[126]Alexi Marcoux, 2003, "A Fiduciary Argument Against Stakeholder Theory," *Business Ethics Quarterly.,* 13(1), pp. 1–24

[127]K. E. Goodpaster, 1991, "Business Ethics and Stakeholder Analysis," *Business Ethics Quarterly,* 1(1), pp. 53–73.

[128]Boatright, 1994.

[129]Richard Marens & Andrew Wicks, 1999 "Getting Real: Stakeholder Theory, Managerial Practice, and the General Irrelevance of Fiduciary Duties Owed to Shareholders," *Business Ethics Quarterly,* 9(2), pp. 273–294.

[130]Goodpaster, 1991, p. 63.

[131]Boatright, 1994.

[132]*Ibid.*, p. 396.

[133]R. Edward Freeman & William Evan, 1990, "Corporate Governance: A Stakeholder Interpretation," *The Journal of Behavioral Economics,* 19(4); Margaret M. Blair, 1995, *Ownership and Control: Rethinking Corporate Governance for the Twenty First Century* (Washington, DC: The Brookings Institution).

[134]Marcoux, 2003

[135]Boatright, 1991, p. 398.

[136]Robert C. Clark, 1985, "Agency Costs versus Fiduciary Duties," in John W. Pratt & Richard J. Zeckhauser (eds.), *Principals and Agents: The Structure of Business,* pp. 55–79.

[137]*Contra* Jensen & Meckling, 1976. "Viewed this way [as a nexus of contracts among individuals], it makes little or no sense to try to distinguish those things which are 'inside' the firm (or any other organization) from those things that are 'outside' of it." p. 311.

[138]Thomas A. Smith, 1999, "The Efficient Norm for Corporate Law: A Neotraditional Interpretation of Fiduciary Duty," *Michigan Law Review,* 98(1), pp. 214–268.

[139]*Ibid.*, p. 243.

[140]*Ibid.*, p. 223.

[141]*Credit Lyonnais Bank Nederland, N.V.* v. *Pathe Comunications Corp.,* No. Civ. A. 12150, 1991 WL 277613, at 1 (Del. Ch. Dec. 30, 1991).

[142]Smith, 1999, p. 223.

[143]*Ibid.*, p. 224.

[144]*Ibid.*, p. 247.

[145]Richard Marens & Andrew Wicks, 1999, "Getting Real: Stakeholder Theory, Managerial Practice, and the General Irrelevance of Fiduciary Duties Owed to Shareholders," *Business Ethics Quarterly,* 9(2), p. 276.

[146]See Marcoux, 2003, for a defense of "morally deep" fiduciary duties.

[147]Marcoux, 2003

[148]Boatright, 1994, p. 404.

[149]Marcoux, p. 19, my emphasis.

[150]Thomas Donaldson, 1989, *The Ethics of International Business* (New York: Oxford University Press).

[151]Freeman, 1984, p 25.

[152]*Ibid.*, p. 46.

[153]See A. K. Sen, 1987, *On Ethics and Economics* (Oxford: Basil Blackwell) for a good discussion of the distinction between "well–being" and "agency" considerations.

[154]Freeman, 1984.

[155]Mark Starik, 1995, "Should Trees Have Managerial Standing? Toward Stakeholder Status for Non–Human Nature," *Journal of Business Ethics,* 14, pp. 207–217.

[156]This chapter is based on my article, "Stakeholder Theory and a Principle of Fairness," *Business Ethics Quarterly,* 7(1), pp. 51–66.

[157]H. L. A. Hart, 1955, "Are There Any Natural Rights?" *Philosophical Review* , 64.

[158]John Stuart Mill, 1859, *On Liberty* (Cambridge: Cambridge University Press, 1989), p. 103f.

[159]John Rawls, 1971, *A Theory of Justice* (Cambridge, MA: The Belknap Press of Harvard University Press), pp. 108–117, 333–355; and Rawls, 1964, "Legal Obligation and the Duty of Fair Play," in S. Hook (ed.), *Law and Philosophy* (New York: New York University Press, 1964); A. John Simmons, 1979,

Moral Principles and Political Obligations (Princeton, NJ: Princeton University Press), pp. 101–142; Kent Greenawalt, 1987, *Conflicts of Law and Morality* (New York: Oxford University Press), pp. 121–158; George Klosko, 1992, *The Principle of Fairness and Political Obligation* (Lanham, MD: Rowman & Little-field Publishers, Inc.); and Klosko, 1987, "Presumptive Benefit, Fairness, and Political Obligation," *Philosophy and Public Affairs,* 16, pp. 241–259; Garrett Cullity, 1995, "Moral Free Riding," *Philosophy and Public Affairs,* 24(1), pp. 3–34; Vincent Maphai, 1987, "The Principle of Fairness," *South African Journal of Philosophy,* 6(3), pp. 73–80; Nora K. Bell, 1978, "Nozick and the Principle of Fairness," *Social Theory and Practice,* 5(1), pp. 65–73; Richard J. Arneson, 1982, "The Principle of Fairness and Free–Rider Problems," *Ethics,* 92, pp. 616–633; Harry J. III Van Buren, 2001, "If Fairness Is the Problem, Is Consent the Solution? Integrating ISCT and Stakeholder Theory," *Business Ethics Quarterly,* 11(3), pp. 481–500; Nien–hê Hsieh, 2000, "Moral Desert, Fairness and Legitimate Expectations in the Market," *The Journal of Political Philosophy,* 8(1), pp. 91–114; Arthur Isak Applbaum, 1999, *Ethics for Adversaries,* (Princeton: Princeton University Press).

[160]Rawls, 1964, pp. 9–10.

[161]This first pass will rely heavily on Simmons's critique of the same work.

[162]Adam Smith, 1976, *The Wealth of Nations,* D. D. Raphael & A. L. Macfie. (eds.) (Oxford: Oxford University Press, 1976). Reprinted Indianapolis, IN: Liberty Classics, 1982.

[163]Rawls, 1971, p. 343.

[164]I owe this point to John Rowan.

[165]See C. McMahon, 1994, *Authority and Democracy* (Princeton: Princeton University Press); Nien–hê Hsieh, 2001, "The Parallel Case Argument for Workplace Democracy," paper presented at the Society for Business Ethics Annual Meeting, Washington, DC.

[166]For a discussion of the implications of property rights for the stakeholder model, see Thomas Donaldson & L.E. Preston, 1995, "The Stakeholder Theory of the Corporation: Concepts, Evidence, and Implications," *Academy of Management Review,* 20(1), pp. 65–91.

[167]See Cullity, 1995, for an excellent summary treatment on free-riding.

[168]John Rawls, 1971, "Justice as Reciprocity," in *Collected Papers* (Cambridge, MA: Harvard University Press), p. 190.

[169]Hart, 1955; Rawls, 1971; and Simmons, 1979.

[170]See, for example, Simmons, 1979.

[171]Robert Nozick, 1974, *Anarchy State, and Utopia* (New York: Basic Books), pp. 90–95.

[172]*Ibid.,* p. 93f.

[173]These represent Simmons's criteria for having accepted a benefit in the sense appropriate to the principle of fairness. See Simmons, 1979, p. 129.

[174]Nozick, 1973, p. 95, Nozick's emphasis.

[175]See Thomas Donaldson & Thomas W. Dunfee, 1999, *Ties That Bind* (Boston: Harvard Business School Press); 1995, "Integrative Social Contracts Theory: A Communitarian Conception of Economic Ethics," *Economics and Philosophy,* 11, pp. 85–112; and 1994, "Toward a Unified Conception of Business Ethics: Integrative Social Contracts Theory," *Academy of Management Review,* 18(2), pp. 252–284.

[176]Donaldson & Dunfee, 1995, *ibid.,* p. 99.

[177]*Ibid.,* p. 101.

[178]On this distinction, see Simmons, 1979, p. 88ff.

[179]Donaldson & Dunfee, 1999, p. 162.

[180]Donaldson & Dunfee, 1995, p. 101.

[181]*Ibid.*, p. 163.

[182]*Ibid.*, pp. 101–117.

[183]See Thomas H. Kuhn, 1971, *The Structure of Scientific Revolutions* (Chicago: University of Chicago Press).

[184]My thanks to R. Edward Freeman for suggesting this point.

[185]R. Edward Freeman, 1994, "The Politics of Stakeholder Theory: Some Future Directions," *Business Ethics Quarterly*, 4(4), pp. 409–422; Edwin M. Hartman, 1996, *Organizational Ethics and the Good Life* (New York: Oxford University Press); Carroll U. Stephens, Virginia W. Gerde, Richard E. Wokutch, & George Watson, 1997, "The Value-Rational Organization: A Rawlsian Perspective on Structure," paper presented at the 1997 Annual Meeting of the International Association of Business and Society.

[186]Jürgen Habermas, 1990, "Discourse Ethics: Notes on a Program of Philosophical Justification," *Moral Consciousness and Communicative Action*, Christian Lenhardt Shierry Weber Nicholsen (trans.) (Cambridge, MA: The MIT Press;); Habermas, p. 66; Habermas's emphasis.

[187]*Ibid.*, 1990, p. 58.

[188]R. Edward Freeman, personal correspondence.

[189]Habermas uses the term monological to describe this sort of analysis.

[190]Jerry M. Calton, 1996, "Legitimizing Stakeholder Voice: The Normative Argument for Institutionalizing Moral Discourse," *1996 Proceedings of the International Association of Business and Society*.

[191]Richard P. Nielson, 1996, *The Politics of Ethics* (New York: Oxford University Press).

[192]The details of the Cadbury example I take from Richard P. Nielson, 1996, *The Politics of Ethics* (New York: Oxford University Press), especially Chapter 8.

[193]Adrian Cadbury, 1987, "Ethical Managers Make Their Own Rules," *Harvard Business Review*, Sept–Oct, pp. 69–73. Quoted in Nielsen, 1996, pp. 125f. Emphasis added.

[194]Nielsen, 1996, p. 129.

[195]A. Cadbury, 1983, "Cadbury Schweppes: More Than Chocolate and Tonic," *Harvard Business Review*, Jan–Feb, pp. 133–144.

[196]Freeman, 1984, p. 31f.

[197]Clarkson, 1994.

[198]This chapter is based on an article published in *Business Ethics Quarterly* entitled, "Stakeholder Legitimacy."

[199]B. K. Burton & C. P. Dunn, 1996, "Feminist Ethics as Moral Grounding for Stakeholder Theory," *Business Ethics Quarterly*, 6(2): 133–148; M. B. E. Clarkson, 1994, "A Risk-Based Model of Stakeholder Theory," Toronto: The Centre for Corporate Social Performance & Ethics; T. Donaldson & T. W. Dunfee, 1999, *Ties That Bind* (Boston: Harvard Business School Press); Thomas Donaldson & L. E. Preston, 1995, "The Stakeholder Theory of the Corporation: Concepts, Evidence, and Implications," *Academy of Management Review*, 20(1), pp. 65–91; William M. Evan & R. Edward Freeman, 1993, "A Stakeholder Theory of the Modern Corporation: Kantian Capitalism," in Tom L. Beauchamp & Norman E. Bowie, (eds.), *Ethical Theory and Business*, 4th ed. (Englewood Cliff's: Prentice Hall); R. Edward Freeman, 1994, "The Politics of Stakeholder Theory: Some Future Directions," *Business Ethics Quarterly*, 4(4), pp. 409–422; Andrew C. Wicks, Daniel R. Gilbert, Jr., & R. Edward Freeman, 1994, "A Feminist Reinterpretation of the Stakeholder Concept," *Business Ethics Quarterly*, 4(4), pp. 475–498.

[200]Donaldson & Preston, 1995, p. 86.

[201]R. K. Mitchell, B. R. Agle, & D. J. Wood, 1997, "Toward a Theory of Stakeholder Identification and Salience: Defining the Principle of Who and What Really Counts," *Academy of Management Review,* 22(4), pp. 853–886.

[202]*Ibid.,* p. 862f, emphasis added.

[203]T. M. Jones, & A. C.Wicks, 1999a, "Convergent Stakeholder Theory," *Academy of Management Review,* 24(2), pp. 206–221, especially at 207n1; T. A. Kochan, & S. A. Rubinstein, 2000, "Toward a Stakeholder Theory of the Firm: The Saturn Partnership," *Organization Science,* 11(4), pp. 367–386.

[204]Mark C. Suchman, 1995, "Managing Legitimacy: Strategic and Institutional Approaches," *Academy of Management Review,* 20(3), pp. 571–610.

[205]Jones & Wicks, 1999a, p. 213.

[206]On the distinction between obligations and duties, see Simmons, 1979.

[207]Clarkson, 1994.

[208]Freeman, 1984; Suchman, 1995.

[209]A. C. Wicks & R. E. Freeman, 1998, "Organization Studies and the New Pragmatism: Positivism, Anti–Positivism, and the Search for Ethics," *Organization Science,* 9(2), pp. 123–140.

[210]Mitchell, Agle, & Wood, 1997, p. 859; emphasis in original.

[211]M. Weber, 1947. *The Theory of Social and Economic Organization* (New York: Free Press). Cited in Mitchell, Agle, & Wood, 1997, p. 865.

[212]Isaiah Berlin, 1969, "Two Concepts of Liberty," *Four Essays on Liberty* (London: Oxford University Press).

[213]Parts of this chapter were published as Robert Phillips & Joel Reichart, 2000, "The Environment as a Stakeholder: A Fairness-Based Approach," *Journal of Business Ethics,* pp. 183–197.

[214]Mark Starik, 1995, "Should Trees Have Managerial Standing? Toward Stakeholder Status for Non–Human Nature," *Journal of Business Ethics,* 14, pp. 207–217.

[215]Donna J. Wood, 1990, *Business and Society* (Glenview, IL: Scott, Foresman & Co.), p. 633.

[216]Starik, 1995, p. 210; Starik's emphasis.

[217]*Ibid.,* p. 210.

[218]*Ibid.,* p. 211. References are to A. B. Carroll, 1989, *Business and Society: Ethics and Stakeholder Management* (Cincinnati: South–Western Publishing Co.); Aldo Leopold, 1949, *A Sand County Almanac* (Oxford: Oxford University Press).

[219]*Ibid.,* p. 212.

[220]*Ibid.,* p. 212.

[221]*Ibid.,* p. 210, Starik's emphasis.

[222]*Ibid.,* p. 211, Starik's emphasis.

[223]*Ibid.,* p. 212.

[224]See, for example, Bryan G. Norton, 1994, "Environmental Ethics and Weak Anthropocentrism," *Environmental Ethics,* 6(2), pp. 131–136, 138–148.

[225]See, for example, Tom Regan, 1985, "The Case for Animal Rights," in Peter Singer (ed.) *In Defense of Animals* (Oxford: Basil Blackwell, Inc.), pp. 13–26; Peter Singer, 1970, "Animal Liberation or Animal Rights," *The Monist.*

[226]Kenneth E. Goodpaster, 1978, "On Being Morally Considerable," *The Journal of Philosophy,* 75, pp. 308–325.

[227]*Ibid.,* p. 310.

[228]Kimberly D. Elsbach & Richard I. Sutton, 1992, "Acquiring Organizational Legitimacy Through Illegitimate Actions: A Marriage of Institu-

tional and Impression Management," *Academy of Management Journal*, 35(4), pp. 699–736.

[229]James Madison, 1787, "Federalist No. 10," in R. P. Fairfield (ed.), *The Federalist Papers* (Baltimore: Johns Hopkins University Press, 1981).

[230]See Robert A. Phillips & Maureen P. Bezold, 1996, "Organizations as the Object of Stakeholder Activism," in Jeanne Logsdon & Kathleen Rehbein (eds.), *Proceedings of the International Association of Business and Society*, pp. 596–601.

[231]Interesting and influential treatments of civil disobedience include H. A. Bedau, 1961, "On Civil Disobedience," *Journal of Philosophy*, 58, pp. 653–661; and John Rawls, 1971, *A Theory of Justice* (Cambridge, MA: The Belknap Press of Harvard University Press), pp. 55–59.

[232]See Plato, "Crito," *The Great Dialogues of Plato*, W.H.D. Rouse (trans.) (New York: Mentor Books, 1984).

[233]Henry David Thoreau, 1849, "Civil Disobedience," in *Civil Disobedience and Other Essays* (New York, Dover Publications, 1993).

[234]Michael Walzer, 1970, "Civil Disobedience and Corporate Authority," *Obligations: Essays on Disobedience, War, and Citizenship* (Cambridge, MA: Harvard University Press), pp. 24–45.

[235]Ray Jones, 1996, "Choosing Moral Duty Over Self–Preservation: An Analysis of Disobedience in Business and Society," in Jeanne Logsdon & Kathleen Rehbein (eds.), *1996 Proceedings of the International Association of Business and Society*, pp. 73–77.

[236]M. L. King, Jr., 1963, *Why We Can't Wait* (New York: Harper & Row), pp. 77–100. Reprinted in Bedau, *Civil Disobedience in Focus*, pp. 68–84.

[237]Friedman, 1982.

[238]Peters & Waterman, 1982.

[239]Albert Z. Carr, 1968, "Is Business Bluffing Ethical?" *Harvard Business Review*, January–February; reprint #68102, p. 4.

[240]Orts & Strudler, 2002.

[241]Berman, Wicks, Kotha, & Jones, 1999.

[242]Orts & Strudler, 2002, p. 219.

[243]R. Edward Freeman, Laura Dunham, & Jeanne Liedtka, 2001, "The Soft Underbelly of Stakeholder Theory: Towards Understanding Community," Darden School Working Paper.

BIBLIOGRAPHY

J. S. Adams, 1963, "Toward an Understanding of Inequity," *Journal of Abnormal and Social Psychology*, 67, pp. 422–436.

Elizabeth Anderson, 1993, *Values in Ethics and Economics* (Cambridge, MA: Harvard University Press).

Arthur Isak Applbaum, 1999, *Ethics for Adversaries* (Princeton: Princeton University Press).

Richard J. Arneson, 1982, "The Principle of Fairness and Free-Rider Problems," *Ethics*, 92, pp. 616–633.

Kenneth Arrow, Samuel Bowles, & Steven Durlauf (eds.), 2000, *Meritocracy and Economic Inequality* (Princeton, NJ: Princeton University Press).

Chester Barnard, 1938/1968, *The Functions of the Executive* (Cambridge, MA: Harvard University Press).

Anthony Barnett, 1997, "Towards a Stakeholder Democracy," in Gavin Kelly, Dominic Kelly, & Andrew Gamble (eds.), *Stakeholder Capitalism* (London: MacMillan Press), pp. 82–98.

H. A. Bedau, 1961, "On Civil Disobedience," *Journal of Philosophy*, 58, pp. 653–661.

Nora K. Bell, 1978, "Nozick and the Principle of Fairness," *Social Theory and Practice*, 5(1), pp. 65–73.

A. A. Berle Jr., 1932, "For Whom Corporate Managers Are Trustees," *Harvard Law Review*, 45.

A. A. Berle Jr., 1931, "Corporate Powers as Powers in Trust, *Harvard Law Review*, 44.

Shawn L. Berman, Andrew C. Wicks, Suresh Kotha, & Thomas M. Jones, 1999, "Does Stakeholder Orientation Matter? The Relationship Between Stakeholder Management Models and Firm Financial Performance," *Academy of Management Journal*, 42(5), pp. 488–506.

Margaret M. Blair, 1995, *Ownership and Control: Rethinking Corporate Governance for the Twenty First Century* (Washington, DC: The Brookings Institution).

John R. Boatright, 1994, "What's So Special About Shareholders," *Business Ethics Quarterly*, 4(4), pp. 393–408.

Norman E. Bowie, 1994, "A Kantian Theory of Capitalism," Ruffin Lecture (Charlottesville, VA: Olsson Center for Applied Ethics).

S. N. Brenner & P. Cochran, 1991, "The Stakeholder Theory of the Firm: Implications for Business and Society Research," Presented at the annual meeting of the International Association of Business and Society, Sundance, UT.

B. K. Burton & C. P. Dunn, 1996, "Feminist Ethics as Moral Grounding for Stakeholder Theory," *Business Ethics Quarterly*, 6(2), pp. 133–148.

John A. Byrne, 1999, *Chainsaw* (New York: HarperBusiness).

Adrian Cadbury, 1987, "Ethical Managers Make Their Own Rules," *Harvard Business Review*, Sept-Oct, pp. 69–73.

Adrian Cadbury, 1983, "Cadbury Schweppes: More Than Chocolate and Tonic," *Harvard Business Review*, Jan-Feb, pp. 133–144.

Jerry M. Calton, 1996, "Legitimizing Stakeholder Voice: The Normative Argument for Institutionalizing Moral Discourse," *1996 Proceedings of the International Association of Business and Society*.

Albert Z. Carr, 1968, "Is Business Bluffing Ethical?" *Harvard Business Review*, Jan-Feb; reprint #68102, p. 4.

John Carter, 1992, "The Rights of Other Corporate Constituencies," *Memphis State Law Review*, 22.

A. B. Carroll, 1993, *Business and Society: Ethics and Stakeholder Management*, 2nd ed. (Cincinnati: South-Western).

A. B. Carroll, 1989, *Business and Society: Ethics and Stakeholder Management* (Cincinnati: South-Western).

Robert C. Clark, 1985, "Agency Costs versus Fiduciary Duties," in John W. Pratt & Richard J. Zeckhauser (eds.), *Principals and Agents: The Structure of Business*, pp. 55–79.

Clarkson Center for Business Ethics, 1999, *Principles of Stakeholder Management: The Clarkson Principles* (Toronto: The Clarkson Center for Business Ethics).

M. B. E. Clarkson, 1995, "A Stakeholder Framework for Analyzing and Evaluating Corporate Social Performance," *Academy of Management Review*, 20(1), pp. 92–117.

M. B. E. Clarkson, 1994, *A Risk-Based Model of Stakeholder Theory* (Toronto: The Centre for Corporate Social Performance & Ethics).

M. B. E. Clarkson, 1991, "Defining, Evaluating, and Managing Corporate Social Performance: A Stakeholder Management Model," in J.E. Post (ed.), *Research in Corporate Social Performance and Policy* (Greenwich, CT: JAI Press), pp. 331–358.

John C. Coffee Jr., 1986, "Shareholders versus Mangers: The Strain in the Corporate Web," *Michigan Law Review*, 85.

James C. Collins & Jerry I. Porras, 1994, *Built to Last: Successful Habits of Visionary Companies* (New York: Harper Collins).

Jason A. Colquitt, Donald E. Conlon, Michael J. Wesson, Christopher O. L. H. Porter, & K. Yee Ng, 2001, "Justice at the Millennium: A Meta-Analytic Review of 25 Years of Organizational Justice Research," *Journal of Applied Psychology*, 86(3), pp. 425–445.

Dan Corry, 1997, "Macroeconomic Policy and Stakeholder Capitalism," in Gavin Kelly, Dominic Kelly, & Andrew Gamble (eds.), *Stakeholder Capitalism* (London: MacMillan Press), pp. 185–202.

Garrett Cullity, 1995, "Moral Free Riding," *Philosophy and Public Affairs*, 24(1), pp. 3–34.

R. Cyert & J. March, 1963, *A Behavioral Theory of the Firm* (Englewood Cliffs, NJ: Prentice Hall).

Norman Daniels (ed.), 1989, *Reading Rawls* (Stanford, CA: Stanford University Press).

Norman Daniels, 1978, "Merit and Meritocracy," *Philosophy and Public Affairs*, 3, pp. 206–223.

Deborah A. DeMott, 1988, "Beyond Metaphor: An Analysis of Fiduciary Obligation," *Duke Law Journal*.

M. Deutsch, 1985, *Distributive Justice* (New Haven, CT: Yale University Press).

M. Deutsch, 1975, "Equity, Equality, and Need: What Determines Which Value Will Be Used As the Basis for Distributive Justice?" *Journal of Social Issues*, 31(3), pp. 137–149.

John Dewey, 1957, *Reconstruction in Philosophy* (Boston: Beacon Press).

E. Merrick Dodd Jr., 1932, "For Whom Are Corporate Managers Are Trustees?" *Harvard Law Review*, 45.

Thomas Donaldson, 1994, "When Integration Fails: The Logic of Prescription and Description in Business Ethics," *Business Ethics Quarterly*, 4(2).

Thomas Donaldson, 1989, *The Ethics of International Business* (New York: Oxford University Press).

Thomas Donaldson, 1982, *Corporations and Morality* (Englewood Cliffs, NJ: Prentice Hall).

Thomas Donaldson & Thomas W. Dunfee, 1999, *Ties That Bind* (Boston: Harvard University Press).

Thomas Donaldson & Thomas W. Dunfee, 1995, "Integrative Social Contracts Theory: A Communitarian Conception of Economic Ethics," *Economics and Philosophy*, 11, pp. 85–112.

Thomas Donaldson & Thomas W. Dunfee, 1994, "Toward a Unified Conception of Business Ethics: Integrative Social Contracts Theory," *Academy of Management Review*, 18(2), pp. 252–284.

Thomas Donaldson & L. E. Preston, 1995, "The Stakeholder Theory of the Corporation: Concepts, Evidence, and Implications," *Academy of Management Review*, 20(1), pp. 65–91.

A. Donnellon & M. Scully, 1994, "Teams, Performance, and Rewards," in C. Hecksher & A. Donnellon (eds.), *The Post-Bureaucratic Organization* (Thousand Oaks, CA: Sage Publications), pp. 63–89.

Albert J. Dunlap, 1996, *Mean Business* (New York: Simon & Schuster).

Ronald Dworkin, 1973, "The Original Position," *University of Chicago Law Review*, 40(3), pp. 500–533.

Kimberly D. Elsbach & Richard I. Sutton, 1992, "Acquiring Organizational Legitimacy Through Illegitimate Actions: A Marriage of Institutional and Impression Management," *Academy of Management Journal*, 35(4), pp. 699–736.

Jon Elster, 1992, *Local Justice* (New York: Russell Sage Foundation).

William M. Evan & R. Edward Freeman, 1993, "A Stakeholder Theory of the Modern Corporation: Kantian Capitalism," in Tom L. Beauchamp & Norman E. Bowie (eds.), *Ethical Theory and Business*, 4th ed. (Englewood Cliffs, NJ: Prentice Hall).

E. F. Fama, 1980, "Agency Problems and the Theory of the Firm," *Journal of Political Economy*, 88, pp. 288–307.

E. F. Fama & M. C. Jensen, 1983, "Agency Problems and Residual Claims," *Journal of Law and Economics*, 26, pp. 327–349.

E. F. Fama & M. C. Jensen, 1983, "Separation of Ownership and Control," *Journal of Law and Economics*, 26, pp. 301–325.

Milton Fisk, 1989, "History and Reason in Rawls' Moral Theory," in Norman Daniels (ed.) *Reading Rawls* (Stanford, CA: Stanford University Press), pp. 53–80.

R. Folger & J. Greenberg, 1985, "Procedural Justice: An Interpretive Analysis of Personnel Systems," in K. Rowland & G. Ferris (eds.), *Research in Personnel and Human Resources Management*, Vol. 3 (Greenwich, CT: JAI Press), pp. 141–183.

Mary Parker Follett, 1995, *Mary Parker Follett-Prophet of Management*, Pauline Graham (ed.) (Boston: Harvard Business School Press).

"Former Sunbeam Chief Exec Settles Hldr Lawsuit for $15M," Dow Jones Newswire, January 14, 2002.

Timothy L. Fort, 1996, "Business as Mediating Institution," *Business Ethics Quarterly*, 6(2), pp. 149–163.

Timothy L. Fort, 1995, "Corporate Constituency Statutes: A Dialectical Interpretation," *Journal of Law and Commerce*, 15, pp. 257–294.

W. C. Frederick, 1994, "From CSR1 to CSR2: The Maturing of Business and Society Thought," Working Paper, University of Pittsburgh, Graduate School of Business, 1978. Reprinted in *Business and Society*, 33(2), pp. 150–164.

William C. Frederick, 1995, *Values, Nature and Culture in the American Corporation* (New York: Oxford University Press).

R. Edward Freeman, 1999, "Divergent Stakeholder Theory," *Academy of Management Review*, 24(2), pp. 233–236.

R. Edward Freeman, 1997, "Political Philosophy, As if Business Matters" presented at the 25th Conference on Value Inquiry.

R. Edward Freeman, 1996, "Understanding Stakeholder Capitalism," *Financial Times* (London Edition), July 18.

R. Edward Freeman, 1994, "The Politics of Stakeholder Theory: Some Future Directions," *Business Ethics Quarterly*, 4(4), pp. 409–422.

R. Edward Freeman, 1984, *Strategic Management: A Stakeholder Approach* (Boston: Pitman Publishing Inc.).

R. Edward Freeman, Laura Dunham, & Jeanne Liedtka, 2001, "The Soft Underbelly of Stakeholder Theory: Towards Understanding Community," Darden School working paper.

R. Edward Freeman & William Evan, 1990, "Corporate Governance: A Stakeholder Interpretation," *The Journal of Behavioral Economics*, 19(4), pp. 337–359.

R. Edward Freeman & Jeanne Liedtka, 1991, "Corporate Social Responsibility: A Critical Approach," *Business Horizons*, 34(4), pp. 92–98.

R. Edward Freeman & Robert A. Phillips, 2002, "Stakeholder Theory: A Libertarian Defense," *Business Ethics Quarterly*, 12(3), pp. 331–349.

Peter A. French, 1979, "The Corporation as a Moral Person," *American Philosophical Quarterly*, 3, pp. 207–215.

Milton Friedman, 1982, *Capitalism and Freedom*, 2nd ed. (Chicago: University of Chicago Press).

Jeff Frooman, 1999, "Stakeholder Influence Strategies," *Academy of Management Review*, 24(2), pp. 191–205.

Andrea Gabor, 2000, *The Capitalist Philosophers* (New York: Times Business).

David Gauthier, 1986, *Morals by Agreement* (New York: Oxford University Press).

D. A. Gioia, 1999, "Practicability, Paradigms, and Problems in Stakeholder Theorizing," *Academy of Management Review*, 24(2), pp. 228–232.

K. E. Goodpaster, 1991, "Business Ethics and Stakeholder Analysis," *Business Ethics Quarterly*, 1(1), pp. 53–73.

K. E. Goodpaster, 1978, "On Being Morally Considerable," *The Journal of Philosophy*, 75, pp. 308–325.

Kent Greenawalt, 1989, *Conflicts of Law and Morality* (New York: Oxford University Press).

Jerald Greenberg, 1990a, "Employee Theft as a Reaction to Underpayment Inequity: The Hidden Cost of Pay Cuts," *Journal of Applied Psychology*, 75(5), pp. 561–568.

Jerald Greenberg, 1990b, "Organizational Justice: Yesterday, Today, and Tomorrow," *Journal of Management*, 16(2), pp. 399–432.

Jerald Greenberg, 1987, "A Taxonomy of Organizational Justice Theories," *Academy of Management Review,* 12(1), pp. 9–22.

Jerald Greenberg, 1987, "Approaching Equity and Avoiding Inequity in Groups and Organizations," in J Greenberg & R. L. Cohen (eds.), *Equity and Justice in Social Behavior* (New York: Plenum), pp. 389–435.

Jerald Greenberg, 1982, "Approaching Equity and Avoiding Inequity in Groups and Organizations," in J. Greenberg & R. L. Cohen (eds.), *Equity and Justice in Social Behavior* (New York: Academic Press), pp. 389–435.

Jerald Greenberg & Robert J. Bies, 1992, "Establishing the Role of Empirical Studies of Organizational Justice in Philosophical Inquiries into Business Ethics," *Journal of Business Ethics,* pp. 433–444.

Jerald Greenberg & C. L. McCarty, 1990, "Comparable Worth: A Matter of Justice," in G. Ferris & K. Rowland (eds.), *Research in Personnel and Human Resources Management,* Vol. 8 (Greenwich, CT: JAI Press) pp. 265–301.

Jürgen Habermas, 1990, "Discourse Ethics: Notes on a Program of Philosophical Justification," *Moral Consciousness and Communicative Action,* Christian Lenhardt and Shierry Weber Nicholsen (trans.) (Cambridge, MA: The MIT Press).

Jürgen Habermas, 1984, 1987, *The Theory of Communicative Action,* Thomas McCarthy (trans.) (Boston: Beacon Press).

Michael Hammer & James Champy, 1993, *Reengineering the Corporation* (New York: HarperBusiness).

Charles Handy, 1992, "Balancing Corporate Power: A New Federalist Paper," *Harvard Business Review,* Nov-Dec, pp. 59–67.

H.L.A. Hart, 1955, "Are There Any Natural Rights?" *Philosophical Review,* 64.

Edwin M. Hartman, 2001, "Moral Philosophy, Political Philosophy, and Organizational Ethics: A Response to Phillips and Margolis," *Business Ethics Quarterly,* 11(4), pp. 673–686.

Edwin M. Hartman, 1996, *Organizational Ethics and the Good Life* (New York: Oxford University Press).

Edwin M. Hartman, 1994, "The Commons and the Moral Organization," *Business Ethics Quarterly,* 4(3), pp. 253–269.

John Hendry, 2001a, "Missing the Target: Normative Stakeholder Theory and the Corporate Governance Debate," *Business Ethics Quarterly,* 11(1), pp. 159–176.

John Hendry, 2001b, "Economic Contracts versus Social Relationships as a Foundation for Normative Stakeholder Theory," *Business Ethics: A European Review,* 10(3), pp. 223–232.

C. W. L. Hill & T. M. Jones, 1992, "Stakeholder-Agency Theory," *Journal of Management Studies,* 29, pp. 131–154.

Nien-hê Hsieh, 2001, "The Parallel Case Argument for Workplace Democracy," paper presented at the Society for Business Ethics Annual Meeting, Washington, DC.

Nien-hê Hsieh, 2000, "Moral Desert, Fairness and Legitimate Expectations in the Market," *The Journal of Political Philosophy,* 8(1), pp. 91–114.

David Hume, 1739, *A Treatise of Human Nature,* L. A. Selby-Bigge (ed.) (Oxford: Clarendon Press, 1960).

Will Hutton, 1995, *The State We're In* (London: Jonathan Cape).

Michael C. Jensen, 2000, "Value Maximization and the Corporate Objective Function," in M. Beer & N. Nohria, *Breaking the Code of Change* (Boston: Harvard Business School Press), pp. 37–58. Reprinted 2002, "Value Maximization, Stakeholder Theory, and the Corporate Objective Function," *Business Ethics Quarterly,* 12(2), pp. 235–256.

M.C. Jensen & W. H. Meckling, 1976, "Theory of the Firm: Managerial Behavior, Agency Costs, and Ownership Structure," *Journal of Financial Economics,* 3, pp. 305–360.

Ray Jones, 1996, "Choosing Moral Duty Over Self-Preservation: An Analysis of Disobedience in Business and Society," in Jeanne Logsdon & Kathleen Rehbein (ed.), *1996 Proceedings of the International Association of Business and Society,* pp. 73–77.

Thomas M. Jones, 1995, "Instrumental Stakeholder Theory: A Synthesis of Ethics and Economics," *Academy of Management Review,* 20(2), pp. 404–437.

Thomas M. Jones & A. C. Wicks, 1999b, "Letter to *AMR* Regarding 'Convergent Stakeholder Theory,'" *Academy of Management Review,* 24(4), pp. 621–623.

Thomas M. Jones & A. C. Wicks, 1999a, "Convergent Stakeholder Theory," *Academy of Management Review,* 24(2), pp. 206–221.

Daniel Kahneman, Jack L. Knetsch, & Richard Thaler, 1986, "Fairness and the Assumptions of Economics," *Journal of Business,* 59(4), pp. S285–S300.

Daniel Kahneman, Jack L. Knetsch, & Richard Thaler, 1986, "Fairness as a Constraint on Profit Seeking: Entitlements in the Market," *The American Economic Review,* 76(4), pp. 728–741.

Michael Keeley, 1988, *A Social Contract Theory of Organizations* (Notre Dame: University of Notre Dame Press).

Gavin Kelly, Dominic Kelly, & Andrew Gamble (eds.), 1997, *Stakeholder Capitalism* (New York: St. Martin's Press).

M. L. King, Jr., 1963, *Why We Can't Wait* (New York: Harper & Row), pp. 77-100. Reprinted in Bedau, *Civil Disobedience in Focus,* pp. 68–84.

George Klosko, 1992, *The Principle of Fairness and Political Obligation* (Lanham, MD: Rowman & Littlefield Publishers, Inc.)

George Klosko, 1987, "Presumptive Benefit, Fairness, and Political Obligation," *Philosophy and Public Affairs,* 16, pp. 241–259.

T. A. Kochan & S. A. Rubinstein, 2000, "Toward a Stakeholder Theory of the Firm: The Saturn Partnership," *Organization Science,* 11(4), pp. 367–386.

Thomas Kuhn, 1970, *The Structure of Scientific Revolutions,* 2nd ed. (Chicago: University of Chicago Press).

Robert Kuttner, 1996, "High Stakes Capitalism," *The Washington Post,* April 8, p. A21.

S. LaTour, 1978, "Determinant of Participant and Observer Satisfaction with Adversary and Inquisitorial Modes of Adjudication," *Journal of Personality and Social Psychology,* 36, pp. 1531–1545.

P. Lawrence & J. Lorsch, 1967, *Organization and Environment* (Homewood, IL: R. D. Irwin).

Aldo Leopold, 1949, *A Sand County Almanac* (Oxford: Oxford University Press).

M. J. Lerner, 1982, "The Justice Motive in Human Relations and the Economic Model of Man: A Radical Analysis of Facts and Fictions," in V. Derlega & J. Grezlak (eds.), *Cooperation and Helping Behavior: Theories and Research* (New York: Academic Press), pp. 249–278.

Wai Shun Wilson Leung, 1997, "The Inadequacy of Shareholder Primacy: A Proposed Corporate Regime that Recognizes Non-Shareholder Interests," *Columbia J. of Law and Social Problems,* 30.

G. S. Leventhal, 1980, "What Should Be Done with Equity Theory? New Approaches to the Study of Fairness in Social Relationships," in K. Gergen, M. Greenberg, & R. Willis (eds.), *Social Exchange: Advances in Theory and Research,* (New York: Plenum Press), pp. 27–55.

G. S. Leventhal, 1976, "The Distribution of Rewards and Resources in Groups and Organizations," in L. Berkowitz & E. Walster (eds.) *Advances in Experimental Social Psychology,* Vol. 9 (New York: Academic Press), pp. 91–131.

G. S. Leventhal, J. Karuza, & W. R. Fry, 1980, "Beyond Fairness: A Theory of Allocation Preferences," in G. Mikula (ed.), *Justice and Social Interaction* (New York: Springer-Verlag), pp. 167–218.

E. A. Lind, S. Kurtz, L. Musante, L. Walker, & J. W. Thibaut, 1980, "Procedure and Outcome Effects on Reactions to Adjudicated Resolution of Conflicts of Interest," *Journal of Personality and Social Psychology,* 39, pp. 643–653.

E. A. Lind & T. Tyler, 1988, *The Social Psychology of Procedural Justice* (New York: Plenum).

Jonathan R. Macey, 1999, "Fiduciary Duties as Residual Claims: Obligations to Nonshareholder Constituencies from a Theory of the Firm Perspective," *Cornell Law Review,* 84, pp. 1266–1281.

Jonathan R. Macey, 1991, "An Economic Analysis of the Various Rationales for Making Shareholders the Exclusive Beneficiaries of Corporate Fiduciary Duties," *Stetson Law Review,* 21.

Jonathan Macey & Miller, 1993, "Corporate Stakeholders: A Contractual Perspective," *University of Toronto Law Review,* 43.

James Madison, 1787, "Federalist No. 10," in *The Federalist Papers,* R.P. Fairfield (ed.) (Baltimore: Johns Hopkins UP, 1981).

Ian Maitland, "The Morality of the Corporation: An Empirical or Normative Disagreement?" *Business Ethics Quarterly,* 4(4), pp. 445–458.

Vincent Maphai, 1987, "The Principle of Fairness," *South African Journal of Philosophy,* 6(3), pp. 73–80.

James G. March & Herbert A. Simon, 1958, *Organizations,* 2nd ed. (Cambridge, MA: Blackwell).

Alexi M. Marcoux, 2003 "A Fiduciary Argument Against Stakeholder Theory," *Business Ethics Quarterly,* 13(1), pp. 1–24.

Alexei M. Marcoux, 2000, "Balancing Act" in J. R. DesJardins, & J. J. McCall (eds.), *Contemporary Issues in Business Ethics,* 4th ed. (Wadsworth), pp. 92–100.

Richard Marens & Andrew Wicks, 1999 "Getting Real: Stakeholder Theory, Managerial Practice, and the General Irrelevance of Fiduciary Duties Owed to Shareholders," *Business Ethics Quarterly,* 9(2), pp. 273–294.

Joshua D. Margolis, 1998, *Dignity in the Balance: Philosophical and Practical Dimensions of Promoting Ethics in Organizations,* Ph.D. dissertation, Harvard University.

Joshua Margolis & James P. Walsh, "Misery Loves Companies: Whither Social Initiatives by Business?" unpublished manuscript.

Joshua Margolis & James P. Walsh, 2001, *People and Profits? The Search for a Link Between a Company's Social and Financial Performance* (Mahwah, NJ: Lawrence Erlbaum).

Morey McDaniel, 1991, "Stockholders and Stakeholders," *Stetson Law Review,* 21.

Christopher McMahon, 1994, *Authority and Democracy* (Princeton: Princeton University Press).

David M. Messick, 1996, "Why Ethics is Not the Only Thing That Matters," *Business Ethics Quarterly,* 6(2), pp. 223–226.

John Stuart Mill, 1848 / 1994, *Principles of Political Economy,* (Oxford: Oxford University Press).

John Stuart Mill, 1859/1989, *On Liberty,* (Cambridge: Cambridge University Press).

David Millon, 1991, "Redefining Corporate Law," *Indiana Law Review,* 24.

Lawrence E. Mitchell, 1992, "A Theoretical and Practical Framework for Enforcing Corporate Constituency Statutes," *Texas Law Review*, 70.

Ronald K. Mitchell, Bradley R. Agle, & Donna J. Wood, 1997, "Toward a Theory of Stakeholder Identification and Salience: Defining the Principle of Who and What Really Counts," *Academy of Management Review*, 22(4), pp. 853–886.

R. T. Mowday, 1987, "Equity Theory Predictions of Behavior in Organizations," in R. M. Steers & L. W. Porter (eds.), *Motivation and Work Behavior*, 4th ed. (New York: McGraw-Hill), pp. 89–110.

David A. Nadler & Michael L. Tushman, 1997, *Competing by Design: The Power of Organizational Architecture* (New York: Oxford University Press).

Thomas Nagel, 1973, "Rawls on Justice," *Philosophical Review*, 82(2), pp. 220–234.

Richard P. Nielson, 1996, *The Politics of Ethics* (New York: Oxford University Press).

Bryan G. Norton, 1994, "Environmental Ethics and Weak Anthropocentrism," *Environmental Ethics*, 6(2), pp. 131–136, 138–148.

Robert Nozick, 1974, *Anarchy State, and Utopia* (New York: Basic Books).

Stuart Ogden & Robert Watson, 1999, "Corporate Performance and Stakeholder Management: Balancing Shareholder and Customer Interests in the U.K. Privatized Water Industry," *Academy of Management Journal*, 42(5), pp. 526–538.

Terry A. O'Neill, 1993, "Employees' Duty of Loyalty and the Corporate Constituency Debate," *Connecticut Law Review*, 25, pp. 681–716.

Eric Orts, 1997, "A North American Legal Perspective on Stakeholder Management Theory," *Perspectives on Company Law*, 2, pp. 165–79.

Eric Orts, 1992, "Beyond Shareholders: Interpreting Corporate Constituency Statutes," *George Washington Law Review*, 61, pp. 14–135.

Jonathan Perraton, 1997, "The Global Economy," in Gavin Kelly, Dominic Kelly, & Andrew Gamble (eds.), *Stakeholder Capitalism* (London: MacMillan Press), pp. 226–237.

T. J. Peters & R. H. Waterman, 1982, *In Search of Excellence* (New York: Harper & Row).

J. Pfeffer & G. Salancik, 1978, *The External Control of Organizations* (New York: Harper and Row).

Kevin Phillips, 1996, "Stakeholder Rebellion: Employees, Consumers Demand Corporate Respect," *USA Today*, March 7, p. 12A.

R. A. Phillips, 2003, "Stakeholder Legitimacy," *Business Ethics Quarterly*, 13(1).

R. A. Phillips, 1997, "Stakeholder Theory and A Principle of Fairness," *Business Ethics Quarterly*, 7(1), pp. 51–66.

R. A. Phillips & Maureen P. Bezold, 1996, "Organizations as the Object of Stakeholder Activism," in Jeanne Logsdon & Kathleen Rehbein (eds.), *Proceedings of the International Association of Business and Society*, pp. 596–601.

R. A. Phillips & J. M. Margolis, 1999, "Toward an Ethics of Organizations," *Business Ethics Quarterly*, 9(4), pp. 619–638.

R. A. Phillips & Joel Reichart, 2000, "The Environment as a Stakeholder: A Fairness-Based Approach," *Journal of Business Ethics*, pp. 183–197.

Plato, "Crito," *The Great Dialogues of Plato*, W.H.D. Rouse (trans.) (New York: Mentor Books, 1984).

Dennis P. Quinn & Thomas M. Jones, 1995, "An Agent Morality View of Business Policy," *Academy of Management Review*, 20(1), pp. 22–42.

John Rawls, 1993, *Political Liberalism* (New York: Columbia University Press).

John Rawls, 1975/1999, "The Independence of Moral Theory," in Samuel Freeman (ed.) *Collected Papers* (Cambridge, MA: Harvard University Press).

John Rawls, 1971/1999, "Justice as Reciprocity," in *Collected Papers*, (Cambridge, MA: Harvard University Press).

John Rawls, 1971, *A Theory of Justice* (Cambridge, MA: The Belknap Press of Harvard University Press).

John Rawls, 1964, "Legal Obligation and the Duty of Fair Play," in S. Hook (ed.), *Law and Philosophy* (New York University Press).

Tom Regan, 1985, "The Case for Animal Rights," in Peter Singer (ed.), *In Defense of Animals* (Oxford: Basil Blackwell, Inc.), pp. 13–26.

Lionel Robbins, 1935, *An Essay on the Nature and Significance of Economic Science* (London: Macmillan).

Richard Rorty, 1994, "Are Assertions Claims to Universal Validity?" published as "Sind Aussagen Universelle Geltungsanspruche?" *Deutsche Zeitschrift fur Philosophie*, 42(6), pp. 975–988.

Timothy J. Rowley, 1997, "Moving Beyond Dyadic Ties: A Network Theory of Stakeholder Influences," *Academy of Management Review*, 22(4), pp. 887–910.

Mike Rustin, 1997, "Stakeholding and the Public Sector," in Gavin Kelly, Dominic Kelly, & Andrew Gamble (eds.), *Stakeholder Capitalism* (London: MacMillan Press), pp. 72–81.

Michael Sandel, 1982, *Liberalism and the Limits of Justice* (Cambridge: Cambridge University Press).

D. A. Schon, 1983, *The Reflective Practitioner: How Professionals Think in Action* (New York: Basic Books).

Amartya Sen, 2000, "Merit and Justice," in Kenneth Arrow, Samuel Bowles, & Steven Durlauf (eds.), *Meritocracy and Economic Inequality* (Princeton, NJ: Princeton University Press).

Amartya Sen, 1987, *On Ethics and Economics* (Oxford: Basil Blackwell).

P. M. Senge, 1990, *The Fifth Discipline* (New York: Doubleday).

Jay M. Shafritz & J. Steven Ott (eds.), 2001, *Classics of Organization Theory*, 5th ed. (Fort Worth: Harcourt College Publishers).

Neil A. Shankman, 1996, "Reframing the Debate Between Agency and Stakeholder Theories of the Firm," *Journal of Business Ethics*, 19, pp. 319–334.

"Shareholder Values," *The Economist*, February 10, 1996, pp. 15–16.

A. Sharplin & L. D. Phelps, 1989, "A Stakeholder Apologetic for Management," *Business and Professional Ethics Journal*, 8(2), pp. 41–53.

Blair H. Sheppard, Roy J. Lewicki, & John W. Minton, 1992, *Organizational Justice: The Search for Fairness in the Workplace* (New York: Lexington Books).

A. John Simmons, 1979, *Moral Principles and Political Obligations* (Princeton, NJ: Princeton University Press).

Peter Singer, 1970, "Animal Liberation or Animal Rights," *The Monist*.

Sloan Stakeholder Colloquy web site, http://www.mgmt.utoronto.ca/~stake/.

Adam Smith, 1790 / 1982, *The Theory of Moral Sentiments*, Part II, Section II, Ch. III. D. D. Raphael & A. L. Macfie (eds.) (Oxford: Oxford University Press, 1976). Reprinted Indianapolis, IN: Liberty Classics.

Adam Smith, 1776/1982, *The Wealth of Nations*, D. D. Raphael & A. L. Macfie. (eds.) (Oxford: Oxford University Press, 1976). Reprinted Indianapolis, IN: Liberty Classics.

Thomas A. Smith, 1999, "The Effiecient Norm for Corporate Law: A Neotraditional Interpretation of Fiduciary Duty," *Michigan Law Review*, 98(1), pp. 214–268.

G. G. Sollars, 2001, "An Appraisal of Shareholder Proportional Liability" *Journal of Business Ethics*, 32(4), pp. 329–345.

Lewis D. Solomon, 1990, "Humanistic Economics: A New Model for the Corporate Constituency Debate," *U. of Cincinnati Law Review*, 59.

Robert C. Solomon, 1993, *Ethics and Excellence: Cooperation and Integrity in Business* (New York: Oxford University Press).

A. A. Sommer Jr., 1991, "Whom Should the Corporation Serve? The Berle-Dodd Debate Revisited Sixty Years Later," *Delaware Journal of Corporate Law*, 16.

David Soskice, 1997, "Stakeholding Yes; the German Model No," in Gavin Kelly, Dominic Kelly, & Andrew Gamble (eds.), *Stakeholder Capitalism* (London: MacMillan Press), pp. 219–225.

"Stakeholder Capitalism," *The Economist*, February 10, 1996, pp. 23–25.

Mark Starik, 1995, "Should Trees Have Managerial Standing? Toward Stakeholder Status for Non-Human Nature," *Journal of Business Ethics*, 14, pp. 207–217.

Carroll U. Stephens, Virginia W. Gerde, Richard E. Wokutch, & George Watson, 1997, "The Value-Rational Organization: A Rawlsian Perspective on Structure," paper presented at the 1997 Annual Meeting of the International Association of Business and Society.

Elaine Sternberg, 2001, "The Stakeholder Concept: A Mistaken Doctrine," *Foundation for Business Responsibilities*.

Elaine Sternberg, 2000, *Just Business* (New York: Oxford University Press).

Elaine Sternberg, 1998, *Corporate Governance: Accountability in the Marketplace* (London: The Institute of Economic Affairs).

Katherine Van Wezel Stone, 1991, "Employees as Stakeholders Under State Nonshareholder Constituency Statutes," *Stetson Law Review*, 21(1).

Mark C. Suchman, 1995, "Managing Legitimacy: Strategic and Institutional Approaches," *Academy of Management Review*, 20(3), pp. 571–610.

Robert I. Sutton & Barry M. Staw, 1995, "What Theory Is Not," *Administrative Science Quarterly*, 40, pp. 371–384.

Phillip E. Tetlock, 2000, "Cognitive Biases and Organizational Correctives: Do Both Disease and Cure Depend on the Politics of the Beholder?" *Administrative Science Quarterly*, 45(2), pp. 293–326.

J. Thibaut & L. Walker, 1975, *Procedural Justice: A Psychological Analysis* (New York: Erlbaum/Halstead).

J. Thompson, 1967, *Organizations in Action* (New York: McGraw Hill).

Henry David Thoreau, 1849/1993, "Civil Disobedience," in *Civil Disobedience and Other Essays* (New York, Dover Publications).

Harry J. Van Buren III, 2001, "If Fairness is the Problem, Is Consent the Solution? Integrating ISCT and Stakeholder Theory," *Business Ethics Quarterly*, 11(3), pp. 481–500.

Mark E. Van Der Weide, 1996, "Against Fiduciary Duties to Corporate Stakeholders," *Delaware Journal of Corporate Law*.

Gary von Strange, 1995, "Corporate Social Responsibility Through Constituency Statutes: Legend or Lie?" *Hofstra Labor Law Journal*, 11(2), pp. 461–497.

Steven M. H. Wallman, 1991, "The Proper Interpretation of Corporate Constituency Statutes and Formulation of Director Duties," *Stetson Law Review*, 21.

Elaine Walster, Ellen Berscheid, & G. William Walster, 1973, "New Directions in Equity Research," *Journal of Personality and Social Psychology*, 25(2), pp. 151–176. Reprinted in Leonard Berkowitz and Elaine Walster (eds.), *Advances in Experimental Social Psychology*, Vol. 9 (New York: Academic Press, 1976), pp. 1–42.

Michael Walzer, 1994, *Thick and Thin* (Notre Dame, IN: University of Notre Dame Press).

Michael Walzer, 1983, *Spheres of Justice* (New York: Basic Books).

Michael Walzer, 1970, "Civil Disobedience and Corporate Authority," in *Obligations: Essays on Disobedience, War, and Citizenship* (Cambridge, MA: Harvard University Press).

A. S. Waterman, 1988, "On the Uses of Psychological Theory and Research in the Process of Ethical Inquiry," *Psychological Bulletin*, 103, pp. 283–298.

Max Weber, 1947, *The Theory of Social and Economic Organization* (New York: Free Press).

Patricia H. Werhane, 1994, "The Normative/Descriptive Distinction in Methodologies of Business Ethics," *Business Ethics Quarterly*, 4(2), pp. 175–180.

Patricia H. Werhane, 1991, *Adam Smith and His Legacy for Modern Capitalism* (Oxford: Oxford University Press).

Patricia Werhane, 1985, *Persons, Rights, and Corporations* (Englewood Cliffs, NJ: Prentice-Hall).

A. C. Wicks & R. E. Freeman, 1998, "Organization Studies and the New Pragmatism: Positivism, Anti-Positivism, and the Search for Ethics," *Organization Science*, 9(2), pp. 123–140.

Andrew C. Wicks, Daniel R. Gilbert Jr., & R. Edward Freeman, 1994, "A Feminist Reinterpretation of the Stakeholder Concept," *Business Ethics Quarterly*, 4(4), pp. 475–498.

Oliver Williamson 1985, *The Economic Institutions of Capitalism* (New York: The Free Press).

O. E. Williamson & J. Bercovitz, 1996, "The Modern Corporation as an Efficiency Instrument: The Comparative Contracting Perspective," in C. Kaysen (ed.) *The American Corporation Today* (New York: Oxford University Press), pp. 327–359.

Donna J. Wood, 1990, *Business and Society* (Glenview, IL: Scott, Foresman & Co.), p. 633.

Michael Young, 1958, *The Rise of the Meritocracy* (London: Thames and Hudson).

INDEX

ABOUT THE AUTHOR

Robert Phillips currently holds joint appointments between the Social/Legal and Management faculty areas at the University of San Diego School of Business Administration. He has been interested in the study of organizational and business ethics since his undergraduate years. As a marketing major and philosophy minor, he was stuck by the fact that the same comment was taken as some form of socialism when uttered among business school students and faculty, and some form of fascism when suggested around philosophy students and faculty. He has been trying to figure out why ever since. During his MBA studies, he was able to take a course in the philosophy department on social justice. This was his first exposure to the work of John Rawls, and it made an impression that has continued to this day. And the perception that he was destined to run a sweatshop among the philosophers and a commune among the business students continued unabated (if not more intensely) during graduate studies.

Upon taking his MBA, he was accepted into the first cohort of Ph.D. candidates at the brand new business ethics program at the University of Virginia's Darden Graduate School of Business Administration. He completed his doctoral program in three years to become the first graduate of this program and *perhaps* the first person in the United States to be granted a Ph.D. explicitly in business ethics from a school of business administration. His work has appeared in the *Business Ethics*

Quarterly, Journal of Business Ethics, Business & Society, and *Teaching Business Ethics* among others. He has previously taught at Georgetown University (McDonough School), the University of Virginia (The McIntire & Darden Schools), and the University of Pennsylvania (The Wharton School.)

Please see next pages for other books
from Berrett-Koehler Publishers

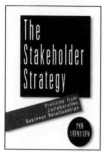

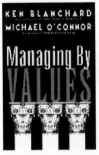

Managing By Values

Ken Blanchard and Michael O'Connor

Based on over 25 years of research and application, *Managing By Values* provides a practical game plan for defining, clarifying, and communicating an organization's values and ensuring that its practices are in line with those values throughout the organization.

Hardcover, 140 pages • ISBN 1-57675-007-8
Item #50078-415 $20.00

Audiotape, 2 cassettes/3 hrs. • ISBN 1-57453-146-8
Item #31468-415 $17.95

True Partnership
Revolutionary Thinking About Relating to Others

Carl Zaiss

The main reason people don't accomplish more is that they don't focus on what really matters when it comes to producing results—the quality of their relationships. In this book, an international business consultant discusses the four mistaken beliefs that keep people from building productive and satisfying relationships: seeing themselves as separate and autonomous, relating to others through power and authority, having an either/or mentality, and seeing the world as fixed and predetermined. Zaiss offers a new framework that can radically transform our relationships and, as a result, our individual effectiveness.

Paperback original, 150 pages • ISBN 1-57675-166-X
Item #5166X-415 $15.95

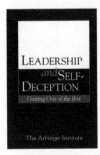

Leadership and Self-Deception
Getting Out of the Box

The Arbinger Institute

Leadership and Self-Deception reveals that there are only two ways for leaders to be: the source of leadership problems or the source of leadership success. The authors examine this surprising truth, identify self-deception as the underlying cause of leadership failure, and show how any leader can overcome self-deception to become a consistent catalyst of success.

Hardcover, 175 pages • ISBN 1-57675-094-9 • Item #50949-415 $22.00
Paperback • ISBN 1-57675-174-0 • Item #51740-415 $14.95

Berrett-Koehler Publishers
PO Box 565, Williston, VT 05495-9900
Call toll-free! **800-929-2929** 7 am-9 pm Eastern Standard Time
Or fax your order to 802-864-7627